Breakthroughs

Breakthroughs

An Integrated Upper Intermediate English Program

Gloria McPherson-Ramirez

Marina Engelking

OXFORD

UNIVERSITY PRESS

OXFORD
UNIVERSITY PRESS

8 Sampson Mews, Suite 204, Don Mills, Ontario M3C 0H5
www.oupcanada.com

Oxford University Press is a department of the University of Oxford.
It furthers the University's objective of excellence in research, scholarship,
and education by publishing worldwide in

Oxford   New York

Auckland   Cape Town   Dar es Salaam   Hong Kong   Karachi
Kuala Lumpur   Madrid   Melbourne   Mexico City   Nairobi
New Delhi   Shanghai   Taipei   Toronto

With offices in
Argentina   Austria   Brazil   Chile   Czech Republic   France   Greece
Guatemala   Hungary   Italy   Japan   Poland   Portugal   Singapore
South Korea   Switzerland   Thailand   Turkey   Ukraine   Vietnam

Oxford is a trade mark of Oxford University Press
in the UK and in certain other countries

Published in Canada by Oxford University Press

Library and Archives Canada Cataloguing in Publication
McPherson-Ramirez, Gloria
Breakthroughs: an integrated upper intermediate English program / Gloria
McPherson-Ramirez, Marina Engelking.

ISBN 978-0-19-543224-4

1. English language—Textbooks for second language learners.   2. English language—Problems,
exercises, etc.   I. Engelking, Marina, 1959–   II. Title.

PE1112.M43 2010   428.2'4   C2009-907123-1

1 2 3 4 — 14 13 12 11

Cover image: Jupiterimages/GettyImages

Oxford University Press is committed to our environment. This book is printed on Forest Stewardship
Council certified paper, harvested from a responsibly managed forest.
Printed and bound in the United States of America.

Acknowledgements

A project of this scope is always a collaborative effort. We thank the professional staff at Oxford University Press Canada, the reviewers of various chapters, our colleagues, students, and our families for their participation and support of this project. Their efforts have enhanced our work immeasurably. Once again, it has been an honour to work with a respected, dedicated, and skilled colleague and friend to create this language program.

Gloria McPherson-Ramirez   *Marina Engelking*

Writing (Student Book & Workbook)	Vocabulary	Pronunciation	Grammar
WB Focus: narrative paragraph SB Activities: superhero adventure story	– finding synonyms for underlined words – identifying adjectives that describe characteristics – completing a text with target words – team game: using target words to describe real or fictional hero	– word stress: suffixes	Adverbs of Manner Grammar in Use: writing a cinquain poem
WB Focus: comparison/contrast paragraph SB Activities: comparison/contrast paragraph of ancient and modern mystery	– completing text with target words – unscrambling letters to form defined words – playing vocabulary tic-tac-toe	– past tense endings	Past Tenses Grammar in Use: writing sentences to narrate the destruction of Pompeii
WB Focus: descriptive paragraph SB Activities: travel brochure	– completing text with target words – matching definitions to words – giving examples of target concepts – completing word webs: word association – labelling map with target words	– linking	Quantifiers Grammar in Use: making T/F quiz using quantifiers
WB Focus: persuasion paragraph SB Activities: report-style paragraph about online youth around the world	– adding vowels to complete target words – completing a crossword – completing a word form chart – writing statements about teen media use using target words	– numbers and expressions of measurement	Reported Speech Grammar in Use: creating and role playing a dialogue
WB Focus: expository paragraph SB Activities: complaint letter	– assigning target words to category headings – choosing statements that explain meaning – writing and role playing a guided dialogue	– linking	Gerunds and Gerund Phrases Grammar in Use: creating a "buyer beware" brochure

Writing (Student Book & Workbook)	Vocabulary	Pronunciation	Grammar
WB Focus: process paragraph SB Activities: taking notes from a crime scene	– assigning target words to category headings – completing text with target words – summarizing a crime story using target words	– sentence stress	Passive Voice Grammar in Use: sharing a story about a solved crime
WB Focus: cause/effect paragraph SB Activities: paraphrased and direct quotes from texts	– choosing words with a similar meaning – agreeing or disagreeing with statements that use the target words – completing a word form chart – reading example situations to identify target words	– contractions	Unreal/Real Conditionals Grammar in Use: interviewing a partner using target words
WB Focus: comparison/contrast paragraph SB Activities: emailing a response to a friend's email; online dating profile	– identifying target words as having a positive or negative meaning – matching words with opposite meanings – completing sentences with target words – choosing qualities you desire in a partner and comparing with a classmate	– intonation: yes/no and information questions	Adjective Clauses Grammar in Use: discussing the ideal partner based on your personal goals and personality traits
WB Focus: narrative paragraph SB Activities: narrating a personal early school experience	– completing sentence text with two-word verbs – grouping target words that have similar meanings – choosing target words associated with photos	– intonation: yes/no, and information questions	Information Questions Grammar in Use: brainstorming questions about a topic of interest
WB Focus: definition paragraph SB Activities: writing song lyrics	– completing a crossword puzzle – completing sentences with target words – creating and presenting a personal culture collage using target words	– minimal pairs: a/the	Articles Grammar in Use: writing a paragraph about child-raising practices in your home culture

Introduction

Welcome to *Breakthroughs*, a stimulating, theme-based upper intermediate English language program. This communicative, integrated-skills program takes you on a journey of discovery through the landscape of English, developing skills in reading, writing, listening, speaking, and pronunciation. Unlike many other language texts which focus primarily on controlled practice and communicative activities, this program encourages you to "break through" the confines of traditional approaches to language learning to develop the knowledge and skills you need to think creatively in English.

Theories about how best to develop language skills abound in the academic literature. We believe that one key to learning any subject successfully lies in motivation. We have built the *Breakthroughs* program around themes that are not only current and relevant, but also interesting and thought-provoking. Each unit begins with a stimulating visual, quiz, puzzle, or discussion activity that introduces the unit theme and motivates you to actively engage with the content that follows. A variety of provocative and creative individual, pair, team, and class exercises in the four skill areas then guide you through activities, which activate your attention to the function and form of language. The reading activities focus on valuable skills such as skimming, scanning, predicting, inferring, and reading charts and graphs, and are built around readings taken from various sources including poetry, personal essays, academic texts, and the Internet. Fun and inspiring listening activities include mini-lectures, interviews, discussions, interviews, and popular songs. The writing activities in each unit offer practice in functional and academic writing from adventure stories, online posts, brochures, advertisements, and emails to paraphrases and paragraphs for specific purposes. A complete academic writing program is built into the accompanying student Workbook. *Breakthroughs* also places a strong emphasis on developing effective speaking skills. Lively speaking activities include playing games, designing surveys, role-plays, oral presentations, and conversations that engage you in a variety of informal and formal communication situations found in daily and academic life. Pronunciation activities throughout the Student Book provide useful support for developing speaking and listening skills. In addition to developing the more traditional language skills, *Breakthroughs* encourages the expression of creative thinking. The program includes unique themes, such as Ethics and Creativity, and the perspective offered on each theme challenges your thinking on these topics, offering real depth. Many activities have a Thinking outside the Box component, a unique feature of this text, which encourages you to think in non-traditional ways. These sections also act as a springboard to exploring issues at a broader, more innovative and sophisticated level. The units in Breakthroughs draw on both Canadian and international references. Each unit's Snapshot of Canada provides a short, interesting theme-related cultural reference. Two chapters are dedicated entirely to the geography, life, and culture of Canada

The aim of *Breakthroughs* is to build communicative competence at an upper intermediate level, although vocabulary-building and grammar—two areas often neglected in other upper-level English texts—are also included. You will not only build your vocabulary, but learn strategies that will allow you to continue to broaden your word power beyond the scope of this text. The Grammar Focus in each unit provides short and clear explanations of the meaning and structure of the target grammar point along with useful exercises that lead you to communicate effectively using standard English grammar. More detailed explanations of all target grammar points are found in the Appendix of the Student Book for easy reference and study. Finally, each unit ends with a Unit Reflection, an activity that serves to summarize the unit and that prompts you to integrate and apply the knowledge and skills you have practised. The sequence of skills practised within each unit changes, and teachers may select to do all or only some of the activities or sections. The units have been designed to either stand alone or be followed in any sequence

A student Workbook, Audio CDs, and an online Teacher's Resource accompany the *Breakthroughs* student text. Ideal for homework, the Workbook provides further practice in, and expansion of, concepts learned in the Student Book, and includes an academic writing program that guides you through the writing process from pre-writing tasks to paragraph writing for various rhetorical modes. In addition to providing further practice in the vocabulary introduced in the Student Book, the Workbook also builds vocabulary with a focus on the Academic Word List. This focus prepares you specifically for successful communication in college, university, and the work place. Each unit of the Workbook provides a comprehensive focus on 10 word families found in the Academic Word List that arise from the unit readings. A complete answer key for all activities is provided. The Audio CDs offer important listening practice with an emphasis on developing effective listening strategies. Pronunciation activities and some grammar and reading practice are also included on the Audio CDs. The online Teacher's Resource includes a complete answer key to the Student Book activities, the audio script of all listening material, and other support material. Journeying through the landscape of English is challenging and exciting. With the *Breakthroughs Upper Intermediate* English Program, we believe your journey will be encouraging, provocative, and enjoyable.

Gloria McPherson-Ramirez
Marina Engelking

Unit 1
Hero to the Rescue!

DISCUSSION

1. Why do people love superheroes?

2. Of all the superheroes you know of, who in your opinion is the best? Why?

3. What makes a great superhero?

Listening

AND A LEAN, SILENT FIGURE SLOWLY FADES INTO THE GATHERING DARKNESS, AWARE AT LAST THAT IN THIS WORLD, WITH GREAT POWER THERE MUST ALSO COME -- GREAT RESPONSIBILITY!

AND SO A LEGEND IS BORN AND A NEW NAME IS ADDED TO THE ROSTER OF THOSE WHO MAKE THE WORLD OF FANTASY THE MOST EXCITING REALM OF ALL!

Before You Listen

1. Look at the comic above. What superhero does this comic show? What impression does the scene and the way the character is standing give?
2. The comic says, "With great power there must also come . . . great responsibility." What do you think this means?

Listening for the Main Idea

Listen to Stan Lee, the creator of Spider-Man, talk about the superhero's character. State the main idea.

Listening for Specific Information

Stan Lee states his beliefs about responsibility. Listen to Lee's explanation again and fill in the missing words:

"Responsibility is always doing what has to be done, what's 1 _____ of you, and what should be done to the best of your 2 _____. . . .

"If you have the ability to do something, and the something should be done is 3 _____ _____ _____ to do, then you have the 4 _____ to do it. . . ."

"You know 5 _____ is so incredibly important because it involves everything. If you cheat on your exam, you're only hurting yourself because your responsibility is to learn that subject. You know most of us don't have a superpower, but we all have 6 _____ to do the right thing. We all have opportunities to make a 7 _____. If everybody treated other people the way they want to be treated that would mean everybody would have a great 8 _____ _____ _____ because when you think about it we are all responsible for our fellow man."

For Discussion

1. Stan Lee took an ordinary character and gave him superpowers, as well as some character flaws. Why do you think he did this?
2. Why does something bad or tragic have to happen before people take action?

Thinking outside the Box

Look at the cartoon below. How does it relate to what Stan Lee talked about?

LIFE ON EARTH   by Ham

BAH - WHY BOTHER?

Reading

Before You Read

Read the title, section headings, and the first sentence of each paragraph. Look at the picture. What information do you expect to read about in the story? What do you already know about this topic? Share your thoughts with two other people.

Superheroes

Superhero to the Rescue

A woman with a baby in her arms appears at the third-floor window of the burning building. *"Help me. Somebody help me. Save my baby,"* she screams in terror. People below look up in horror, powerless to help the trapped mother and child. One person points upwards and says, *"Look up in the sky. It's a bird. It's a plane. It's Superman!"* And then, just in time, my heroic caped crusader flies down and rescues the trapped pair from the raging fire. He puts them safely on the ground. The crowd cheers. Once again, Superman has saved the day.

---

caped crusader: champion, hero in a costume
raging: intense and wild

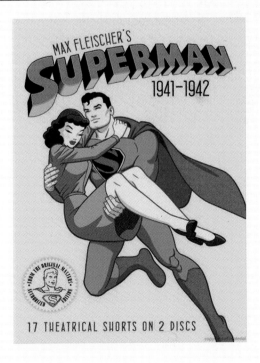

Heroic Qualities

You are probably wondering why someone my age loves reading superhero stories so much. I admit that I've loved reading superhero comics and watching the cartoons since I was a child. As a kid, I even wanted to be a superhero when I grew up. Superheroes are awesome. They seem to be invincible. They show great courage when fighting evildoers and never let anything stand in their way. They willingly make great sacrifice in their personal lives to save mankind from the evil around us. They face danger as though they have no fear. They understand the responsibility that their abilities give them and are committed to doing the right thing. Their selfless devotion to making the world a better place to live is so admirable. Few individuals actually choose to do things if they can't profit from the action themselves, but superheroes do. Superheroes have so many qualities that I admire in ordinary individuals but magnified many times. They may not always win, but they always return to fight another day.

---

awesome: incredible
invincible: unbeatable
mankind: human race
magnified: made larger

Sources of Superpowers

So apart from their heroic qualities, what is it about these superheroes that have made children love and admire them? They usually have amazing physical skills and are able to control elements of nature such as fire or water. These superpowers definitely appeal to kids. Most superheroes' powers come from four major origins. Some superheroes were actually born with their superpowers. The mutants in the X-Men series were born with their powers. Wolverine, for example, has animal-like powers. He is known for his retractable bone claws and his amazing self-healing powers that allow him to recover when attacked by the enemy. Others got their powers as a result of an accident or experiment that went wrong. Peter Parker (Spider-Man) got his spider-like skills after being bitten by a radioactive spider. Bruce Banner's superhero identity, the Hulk, developed as a result of a scientific experiment that altered his DNA with gamma radiation. Some superheroes have superpowers because they are aliens from other planets. Superman is from the planet Krypton. He arrived on earth as a baby after his planet was destroyed. His superpowers developed as he grew older. The fourth source of superpowers is special high-tech gadgets that individuals have developed to help them fight crime. Batman has his super-powered computer, car, boat, helicopter, and motorcycle, bat shield, and countless other gadgets. Iron Man has his super suit that deflects bullets and allows him to fly. Regardless of the source of the superheroes' abilities, they always have some characteristics that make us think they could be one of us.

---

retractable: able to go back in
radioactive: giving off energy which is harmful
deflect: make something change direction

Ordinary Lives

Many of the superheroes live like ordinary citizens. Clark Kent was raised by Jonathan and Martha Kent, a couple who have strong morals and values. As an adult he becomes a reporter for the *Daily Planet*. His job lets him hear breaking news and gives him a reason to be at crime scenes. There he secretly goes into a phone booth, changes his clothes, and comes out as the man in blue tights and red cape with the large S on his chest—Superman. Spider-Man's alter ego

also works for a newspaper—the *Daily Bugle*. He is Peter Parker, a lonely, awkward teenager. He is struggling as a photographer to make money to support himself and his Aunt May. As Spider-Man he tries to rid the world of criminals in memory of his uncle who was murdered. Bruce Wayne (Batman) is a wealthy industrialist. He witnessed the terrible murder of his parents as a child. Like Peter Parker, he decided to dedicate his life to fighting crime. According to the Oxford dictionary, a superhero is *"a person or fictional character with extraordinary heroic attributes."* It is someone who has courage, takes risks, and often makes personal sacrifices for the good of others. Whether they have natural talents that strong role models have taught them to use for good or whether a tragic experience has motivated them to take on a heroic role, these characters show us that ordinary people can fight injustice. It is possible for us to be like them.

---

morals: beliefs about right and wrong
alter ego: a second identity
awkward: shy, uncomfortable
industrialist: owner of a large factory

Current Appeal

The fantastic scenes that I imagined as I read my superhero comics as a child are now possible to create thanks to advances in technology. Movie producers are able to use amazing special effects and computer generated images (CGI) to realistically show their characters and superpowers. There is a whole new generation of superhero fans because of the popularity of television series such as *Smallville* and *Heroes*. Totally animated superhero movies such as *The Incredibles* and *Monsters vs Aliens* have been very popular with children. Hollywood loves the superhero and has produced one blockbuster after another. The Spider-Man series has made hundreds of millions of dollars. *Men in Black*, *Superman Returns*, *The Dark Knight*, *Hulk,* and *Iron Man* are just some of the recent and extremely successful superhero movies. They have popular movie stars that we can relate to as our favourite superheroes. These movies bring back memories of a simpler time. These superhero movies offer us hope. We think about these super-heroes as if they could possibly exist today. When we feel that the world is spinning out of control, these superheroes make us optimistic that someone with extraordinary strength, courage and ability will come along and rescue us.

---

optimistic: hopeful

"I don't care how many people you rush off to save on your own time, 'Lightning Man,' but while you're here, you're Bob Clark of accounts and you don't leave your desk till 5:30!"

Comprehension Check

Match the idea on the left with the reason on the right. More than one answer may be possible.

1. Superman has the ability to save people.
   ___*j*___

2. Superheroes do not fight crime for money. _____

3. Some superheroes are considered to be mutants. _____

4. Some individuals do not have superpowers, but they are still superheroes. _____

5. Superheroes generally need to have ordinary jobs. _____

6. Some superheroes did not always want to be superheroes. _____

7. Superhero movies are much better now than in the past. _____

8. The current superhero movies make a lot of money. _____

9. Superhero movies offer us hope. _____

10. We admire superheroes. _____

a) Sometimes something terrible happens in the person's life that causes them to take on the superhero role.

b) We like to think that it is possible for someone to rescue us.

c) We pay to see movie stars play our favourite superheroes.

d) Superheroes have many qualities and characteristics that we think are great.

e) They have high-tech gadgets that make them superheroes.

f) The use of special effects and CGI means the producers can show special abilities and locations.

g) They had their superpowers from birth and were born on Earth.

h) The jobs let them find out about crimes and be at crime scenes.

i) They are selfless and fight for their beliefs.

j) He can fly into burning buildings and use his superpowers.

For Discussion

1. Popular comics that were created in the 1940s had superheroes that were generally white and male. Why do you think this was?
2. How has the image of the superhero changed in the last decade?

3. Movies such as *Hancock* and *The Dark Knight* show some of the dark or negative characteristics of superheroes. What are some of these characteristics? Why is the superhero's individual struggle with good and evil important?
4. Why do superhero stories usually have a villain that represents evil?

SNAPSHOT OF CANADA 📷

Did you know that the great American hero, Superman, was, in fact, a Canadian creation?

Toronto-born cartoonist, Joe Shuster, came up with the idea of a "strange visitor from another planet with powers and abilities far beyond those of mortal men" with his buddy, Jerry Siegel, when the pair was only seventeen years old.

According to Canadian novelist Mordecai Richler, Shuster's Superman is a perfect expression of the Canadian psyche. The mighty "man of steel" hides his extraordinary strength, speed, and superhuman powers under the bland, self-effacing guise of the weak and clumsy Clark Kent. He is a hero who does not take any credit for his own heroism, a glamorous figure in cape and tights who is content to live his daily life in horn-rimmed glasses and brown suits.

Vocabulary

Exercise A

Find a synonym in the reading for the underlined words related to superheroes. Identify if the word or phrase is a noun (n), verb (v), or adjective (adj).

Superhero to the Rescue

1. Superheroes always try to <u>save</u> mankind from evil-doers.

Heroic Qualities

2. Superheroes often have <u>given up something they value</u> in order to help mankind.

Sources of Superpowers

3. Superheroes have <u>abilities to do</u> things that ordinary people don't have.
4. Their powers are simply <u>remarkable</u>—average humans can't do those things.

Ordinary Lives

5. Superheroes try to catch <u>people who have done something illegal</u>.
6. They show <u>bravery</u> when faced with danger.
7. When they see <u>unfair treatment of people</u>, they try to make things right.

Current Appeal

8. We look for someone with <u>exceptional</u> skills to rescue us.

Exercise B

Many ordinary people exhibit heroic qualities even though they do not have superpowers. Read these statements describing everyday heroes. Underline the adjectives that describe their characteristics. Look up the meaning of any adjectives that are unfamiliar to you.

a) Mother Teresa's selfless and persistent dedication to the poor of India and surrounding countries improved the lives of many people.

b) Many people think the Dalai Lama is honest. He is well-respected and a hero to his people.

c) The physician Norman Bethune was very innovative. He developed the first mobile blood transfusion unit to be used on the battlefield, which saved many lives.

d) Many people feel that Che Guevara was a hero because he was dedicated to helping Latin Americans fight for their rights.

e) Fans describe Oprah Winfrey as trustworthy. She has used her wealth and influence to improve the lives of many underprivileged people.

Exercise C

The Life of a Superhero

Complete the text using the appropriate words from the box. Use each word only once.

```
powers              sacrifices

criminals           extraordinary

injustice
```

By day, my superhero works in an ordinary job. A When he hears about a crime or a (n) 1 _____ taking place, he slips away unnoticed and changes into his superhero costume. B Before the 2 _____ can escape, he uses his powers to stop them. C His superpowers are 3 _____. D He could easily use these superpowers for his own benefit, but instead he 4 _____ his own interests for the good of others. He moves about the city quickly E and arrives on the scene before anyone sees him coming. The evil villains do not know what is happening, and before they know it, they have been captured. F Although he has helped so many people, he can't let anyone know his secret identity. He is quite lonely. He has few friends. He also worries about enemies who want to stop his good deeds. G But he knows he has a responsibility to use his 5 _____ against the forces of evil. Each day he does some heroic thing to make our world a better place. H

Vocabulary in Use

Who Am I?

Work in pairs. Choose one real or fictional hero. Write five sentences that describe your hero (without naming the hero) and write them on separate strips of paper. Use words from Exercise A or B above in each sentence.

Example:

1. He is amazing. During his first year as president, he won a Nobel Peace Prize.

2. He was a well-respected lawyer and politician before he was elected president of the United States.

3. Many people were optimistic that he would make great changes while president.

4. He is also a dedicated husband and father of two daughters.

5. His election as president was extraordinary because he was the first Black president.

Correct Answer: US president Barack Obama

Play: Divide into two teams. The goal is for your team to get the most points. One pair from Team A will select one sentence from their pile and read it to their teammates, who have twenty seconds to make one guess. If the correct answer is not given, the pair reads the next clue. This pattern is repeated until all clues have been read.

Stealing: The other team can steal at any point. If members from the other team think they know the answer, they yell out "steal" and give their response. If they are correct, they get the points. (See scoring on page 8.) The opposing team is only allowed one chance to steal per hero, so if the team is wrong, it can't steal again.

Play now switches to Team B. One pair in the team reads clues to their teammates while the other team tries to steal.

Scoring: Your team receives one point for each clue sentence that includes a vocabulary word from Vocabulary Exercise A or B.

If the correct answer is guessed after one clue, 5 points are awarded; two clues, 4 points; three clues, 3 points; four clues, 2 points; and five clues, 1 point.

Example: If your team wrote five clues that each included one of the target words **and** your team mates guessed the correct answer on the first clue, you would receive 5 + 5 = 10 points.

Grammar Focus

Exercise A

Look at the following sentences. Underline the word in each sentence that indicates *how* something happened or was done. Where is this word located in the sentence (before/after the verb/object **or** beginning of the sentence)?

1. Shaktiman, a popular superhero in India, transported his body instantly to another location.
2. Spider-Man swung swiftly through the city on his spiderwebs.
3. Incredibly, Iron Man jetted across the sky as fast as a plane.
4. Darna fearlessly faces man-made weapons because she can't be harmed by them.
5. Criminals consistently told the truth when they were tied up with Wonder Woman's golden lasso.
6. Batman monitors the sky carefully for the bat signal, which indicates he is needed to fight crime.
7. China's Monkey King somersaulted skillfully onto a cloud and raced across the sky.
8. Clark Kent deliberately hid his superhero identity from Lois Lane.
9. El Gato Negro expertly used his wrestling and martial arts skills to fight against evildoers.
10. Goku transformed speedily into a powerful monkey.

Exercise B

1. List the adverbs that you underlined in Exercise A. Write the adjective that corresponds to each adverb.

- Identify the suffix that is added to adjectives to make them adverbs.
- Identify the endings on adjectives that had to change to form adverbs.

2. What spelling rules can guide you when forming adverbs? Check page 144 for the correct answer.

> **Adverbs of Manner**
> - An adverb of manner indicates *how* something happens or is done.
> - Most adverbs end in *–ly* and can be found anywhere in the sentence; however, most adverbs of manner are usually found after an intransitive verb or the direct object of a transitive verb
>
> **Example:**
>   verb   adverb
> - The Hulk walked slowly.
>   verb   d.o.   adverb
> - The pilot landed the plane safely.

Exercise C

Adverbs add more information to the verb. Underline the verb in the following sentences. Circle the direct object if there is one. Add an adverb to indicate how the action was done.

1. Batman drove the Batmobile to the robbery that was in progress.
2. Goku fought his enemies.

3. Superman changed into his red and blue costume to respond to the fire.

4. The criminals robbed the bank.

5. El Gato Negro climbed the building.

6. Peter Parker sacrificed his own interests so he could save the world from criminals.

7. Mr. Fantastic stretches his body.

8. The Invisible Woman controls her powers.

If you want to intensify an adverb (make it stronger), you can add words like **very**, **too**, **so**, **really**, and **extremely** before it. If you want to qualify (limit) an adverb, you can add words like **quite**, **rather**, **fairly**, **somewhat**, and **a bit** before it.

Examples:

John played **very** energetically.
He drove **somewhat** slowly.

*Don't overuse intensifiers or qualifiers. In writing it is often better to use a precise adverb.

Pronunciation Power

Word Stress

The suffix –ly does not change the word stress of the root word. This means that the stress for an adverb ending in –ly will be exactly the same as the stress for the adjective that is the root of the word.

Example:

peace/ful (adj.)

peace/ful/ly (adv.)

safe (adj.)

safe/ly (adv.)

Listen to the adjective/adverb pairs from Grammar Exercise B. Mark the syllable stress and practise saying both forms.

Grammar in Use

Superhero Poetry

On the first line write the name of a superhero.

On the second line write **two adjectives** joined by *and* to describe this superhero.

On the third line write a **verb** and an **adverb** to describe this superhero in action.

Start the fourth line with **as if** or as **though** followed by a comparison.

On the final line write a descriptive phrase describing the superhero.

Example:

> Superman
> *fast and strong*
> *arriving quickly*
> *as though he could travel through time*
> *my caped crusader*

Speaking

In pairs: Tell each other about a popular superhero in your culture. Use the text in Vocabulary, Exercise C—The Life of a Superhero on page 7 as your story base. Insert the following details. If your hero is female, you may have to change some words.

A Describe your superhero's job.

B Describe the costume your superhero wears. Give details about the colour, style, and accessories.

C Describe their superpowers.

D Describe the origin of their superpowers.

E Describe how the superhero moves about the city. Do they use a special vehicle? Do they have a special ability that allows them to move about?

F Describe how the superhero captures bad guys. What gadgets or powers do they use? What do they do with the criminals once they have been caught?

G Explain how enemies can stop your superhero. What can harm them? Is it exposure to something?

H Describe what your hero does to make the world a better place.

Writing

Write about a new adventure for the superhero you described in the Speaking activity. Use the following outline to tell the story:

- What is your superhero's name?
- What was the superhero doing when the problem or crime occurred?
- What did they do when they heard about the problem or crime?
- What bad circumstance or evil enemy did they have to overcome?
- How did they use their powers to do this?
- What happened in the end?

Unit Reflection

Choose a real-life hero. Discuss the person's achievements and personal qualities. Compare the real hero with a popular superhero. In what ways are they similar and different? What does this comparison teach you about human life?

Unit 2
Ancient Secrets Revealed

Cliffcrest 416 396 8916
Toronto Public Library

User ID: 2 ********* 2900

Date Format: DD/MM/YYYY

Number of Items: 1

Item ID:37131133700161
   Title:Breakthroughs [sound recording]
an integrated upper intermediate
English program
Date due:18/09/2013

Telephone Renewal# 416 393 5505
www.torontopubliclibrary.ca
Wednesday, August 28, 201 12:40 PM

DISCUSSION

1. Which ancient secrets do we know the answe...

2. Which ancient secrets are still a mystery?

Listening

Before You Listen

You will hear three short lectures about ancient objects that have been discovered. One strategy that improves your ability to understand lectures and take effective notes is to think about what you already know about the topic. Look at the pictures. What do you know about them? What remains a mystery?

Stonehenge

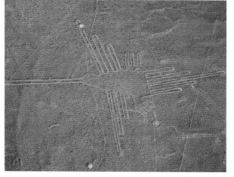

Nazca Lines

Terra Cotta Warriors

Listening for Specific Information

Take notes as you listen. For each lecture, use either point-form notes or a mind map to record key words that explain the following:

1. what the ancient artifact is;
2. where it is located;
3. when it was constructed;
4. who built it; and
5. the theories about why it was built.

Pyramid

I. What: Structure
   A. Triangular sides coming to point
      1. huge in size
      2. brick or stone
   B. Tomb
      1. pharaohs / important people
      2. treasures

II. Where: Egypt
   A. Giza
   B. West bank of Nile

III. When: Third millennium BCE onwards
   A. most built 2575–2150 BCE

IV. Who
   A. farmers and local workers
   B. aliens from another planet

V. Theories: Purpose and Design
   A. stairway to heaven for the pharaohs
   B. map for aliens

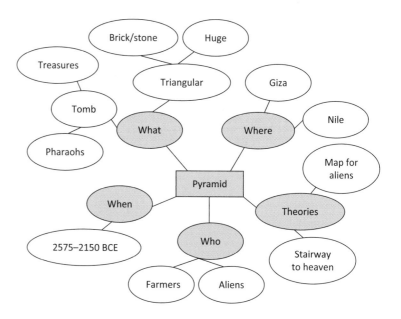

For Discussion

In small groups, discuss ONE of the three lectures. Your teacher may assign you a lecture. Share information from your notes to make a detailed and complete set of notes for the group. Then, form new groups where each member has detailed notes about a different ancient artifact. Use your detailed notes to retell the story of your ancient mystery to the group.

Thinking outside the Box

In groups, choose one of these topics: the ancient mystery of Stonehenge, the Nazca Lines, or the Terra Cotta Warriors. Which explanation of its purpose seems the most reasonable to your group and why? Present the reasons for your choice to your classmates.

Vocabulary

Exercise A

Complete the descriptions of the following using the words listed.

a) *code, rituals, society, secret*

The Knights Templar was an ancient 1. _____ that began in the early twelfth century in France. It was a group of individuals who protected poor travellers who were going to the Holy Land. Later, in addition to fighting, they also developed a financial system. Individuals deposited their money at a Templar house in one city and got a receipt that contained a 2. _____. They could travel safely to another city and exchange the receipt with the secret information at another Templar house to receive their money. The Knights Templar became very rich because anyone who wanted to be a Templar Knight had to give all his possessions to the group. Members also had to perform certain 3. _____ such as wearing a special cord next to their bodies. Many people believe that in addition to great wealth, this society had

4. _____ knowledge of religious treasures. The Knights Templar guarded this knowledge that no one else had very carefully.

b) *speculation, proof, revealed, forgeries*

The Ica Stones of Peru are a collection of approximately fifteen thousand carved rocks that were supposedly found in a cave and date from ancient times. A farmer who claimed that he found them sold the stones to tourists. These stones have carvings which show ancient history, animals, surgery, and glimpses of the future. The farmer never 1. _____ the location where he found the rocks, which led to 2. _____ that the rocks were 3. _____. No 4. _____ that they are real exists. Many now suggest that they are fakes—not ancient artifacts.

c) *conspiracy, mystery, hoax, theory*

Farmers have found strange patterns that have appeared overnight in their fields. The origin of these crop circles remains a 1. _____. One 2. _____ is that the patterns are some sort of communication from another planet. Others believe that the circles are just a 3. _____ and are not real at all. They believe that there is a 4. _____

planned by a group of individuals to trick people into believing that these symbols are the work of aliens from other planets.

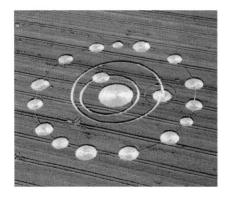

d) *ancient, archeology, excavation*

A professor of 1. _____ from Belgium, who studies ancient objects and their culture, supervised the 2. _____ of the Roman baths found in Sagalassos, an ancient city located in southwestern Turkey. While digging at this site, a team discovered pieces of a marble statue of the Roman emperor Hadrian. He ruled between 117 and 138 CE, and the statue was made during his rule. The 3. _____ statue reveals that Hadrian had a beard. He is the first Roman emperor to be shown with a beard.

Exercise B

Unscramble the letters to form the words defined. Take the letters that appear in ◯ boxes and unscramble them to identify the two-word expression used to describe a belief that some event is the result of a secret plan by a powerful group of people. For example, some people do not believe that Americans actually landed on the moon. They think that the US government made up this story.

1. system used for secret communication:
   DOCE ◻◻◻◻
2. patterns of behaviour regularly performed in a ceremony: TUSRALI ◻◻◻◻◻◻◻
3. a group that meets together regularly because of common interests: COSYTIE ◻◻◻◻◻◻◻
4. kept hidden from others:
   REESTC ◻◻◻◻◻◻
5. guesses about something that is unknown:
   CITPAELOSUN ◻◻◻◻◻◻◻◻◻◻◻
6. things falsely copied to deceive others:
   REFGOSERI ◻◻◻◻◻◻◻◻◻
7. hole dug to uncover old artifacts:
   NTXAOECVIA ◻◻◻◻◻◻◻◻◻◻
8. the study of bones, tools, and artifacts of ancient peoples: GOCHYRLOAE
   ◻◻◻◻◻◻◻◻◻◻◻
9. a way to show that something is true:
   FOPOR ◻◻◻◻◻
10. very old: NAITECN ◻◻◻◻◻◻◻
11. to make something known:
    LEVARE ◻◻◻◻◻◻
12. something that is not known:
    MESRYTY ◻◻◻◻◻◻◻
13. an act meant to trick or deceive:
    XAHO ◻◻◻◻

Vocabulary in Use

Tic Tac Toe

Play the game in groups of three: Students A and B play against each other and Student C is the judge.

1. Student A chooses a square, gives a definition of the word, and uses it in a sentence. Student C can check the answer on page 21. If the definition and the sentence are both correct, Student C awards the square to Student A. If the definition or sentence are incorrect, Student C awards the square to Student B.
2. Now, Student B selects a square. Take turns alternating between Student A and Student B.
3. The game continues until either Student A or Student B has three squares in a row.

ritual

secret

forgery

excavation

proof

mystery

theory

ancient

reveal

Grammar Focus

Exercise A

1In 1886, a man was digging on his uncle's farm near Highgate, Ontario, when he uncovered some very large bones. 2Four years later, two men from Orangeville paid the farmer twenty-five dollars to let them dig around the site and keep whatever they found. 3They dug for a few days and found more than 157 bones belonging to a mastodon. 4The mastodon, a prehistoric animal, walked the Earth 10,500 years ago. 5This was the most complete fossilized skeleton of an extinct animal in North America at that time. 6The bones were shown at fairs and exhibitions across Canada before they mysteriously disappeared. 7The bones turned up years later in the United States and were sold to the

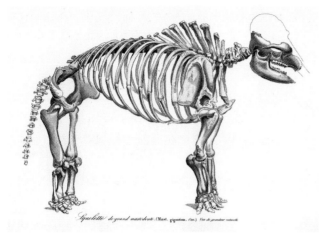

Mastodon skeleton

University of North Dakota. ₈They stayed in storage until two paleontologists assembled the skeleton at the end of the twentieth century. ₉The scientists studied the bones and determined that the mastodon had died after fighting with another beast.

1. Underline all the verbs that indicate past time.
2. In sentence 1, which action happened first—**digging** or **uncovered?**
3. What are the time expressions used in sentences 4 and 5? What tense is used? What is the verb form?
4. In sentence 9, which action happened before the other actions in the sentence? What tense is used to indicate this? What is the verb form?
5. Which sentence describes an action that was in progress when another action happened in the past? What verb tense is used to indicate this? What is the verb form?

Past Time

We can think of actions as having four possible relationships to past time. An action is

1. *at* that time (simple past);
2. in progress *during* that time (past progressive/continuous);
3. *before* that time (past perfect); or
4. in progress *during* and *before* that time (past perfect progressive/continuous).

Exercise B

Fill in the blanks with an appropriate past tense form. Look for signal words and other time clues to help make your decision. Discuss the reasons for your choices with a partner.

Recently, while a woman 1 _____ (clean) the attic of her parents' house in Highgate, she 2 _____ (uncover) some fossilized bones long since forgotten. Someone 3 _____ (wrap) the bones in a newspaper that was dated 1933. The woman 4 _____ (donate) the fossils to the University of Waterloo's Earth Science Museum. Experts at the university 5 _____ (be) able to confirm that the bones, two molars, and a tusk from a lower jaw, 6 _____ (be) from a mastodon that 7 _____ (walk) the Earth more than 10,500 years ago.

A research team from the university 8_____ (think) that the tusk they 9 _____ (receive) from the woman possibly 10 _____ (belong) to the famous Highgate mastodon. Old newspaper stories 11 _____ (report) that excavators in the 1890s 12 _____ (find) only one tusk. The researchers 13 _____ (go) to the location where the farmer 14 _____ (find) the famous bones to check their theory.

Signal Words

When and *while* are words that signal whether an action happens at a specific time (when) or is in progress when another action occurs (while).

Exercise C

Combine the past actions into one sentence. You may need to change tenses to show the time order of the actions and whether actions happened *at that time* or *during that time.*

1. Thousands of people were living in Pompeii, an ancient Roman city in Italy located near Mt. Vesuvius. A volcano erupted.

   When <u>the volcano erupted</u>, thousands <u>of people were living in Pompeii.</u>

2. Inhabitants tried to escape. The molten lava and ash buried them.

While _____, the molten lava and ash _____.

3. In the eighteenth century, workmen dug a foundation for a summer palace for the King of Naples. They rediscovered the ruins of the city.

Workmen _____ while _____.

4. In the nineteenth century, they began to excavate the ruins. They discovered holes in the ash and human remains.

They _____ when they _____.

5. They filled the holes with plaster and let it dry. You could see the shapes and facial expressions of the victims.

When the plaster _____, you _____.

Grammar in Use

Write four or five sentences using the appropriate tenses to tell the story of the destruction and excavation of the city of Pompeii shown in the pictures.

Ancient Pompeii, Italy

Mount Vesuvius erupts, 79 CE

Running for their lives

Victims uncovered

Ruins of Pompeii today

Pronunciation Power

English has two kinds of sounds: voiced and unvoiced. With voiced sounds there is a vibration in the throat.

With unvoiced sounds there is no vibration in the throat.

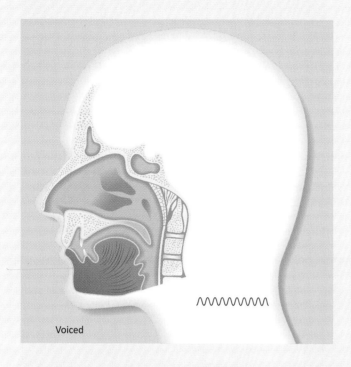

Voiced

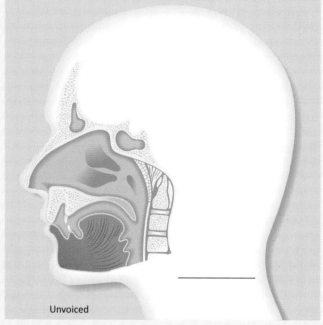

Unvoiced

The regular past tense (V2) and past participle (V3) is formed by adding *–ed* to the base form of the verb. Keep the following in mind:

- Pronounce the *–ed* of the regular past tense as /d/ after voiced sounds. Voiced sounds include all vowels and /b/, /d/, /g/, /j/ (as in judge), /l/, /m/, /n/, /r/, /ð/, /v/, /w/, /ng/, /zh/, and /z/.

  Examples: sta<u>y</u>ed, se<u>w</u>ed, fea<u>r</u>ed, revea<u>l</u>ed,
- Pronounce the *–ed* of the regular past tense as /t/ after a voiceless sound. Voiceless sounds include /f/, /k/, /p/, /s/, /th/, /ch/, and /sh/.

  Example: fa<u>k</u>ed

- Pronounce the *–ed* as /id/ after /t/ or /d/.

  Example: excava<u>t</u>ed

Listen to and repeat the sentences in Grammar Focus, Exercises A and B. Pay careful attention to the pronunciation of the V2 and V3 form of regular verbs. With a partner, take turns reading the sentences.

SNAPSHOPT OF CANADA 📷

Oak Island, a small island off the coast of Nova Scotia, may conceal the world's greatest treasure, that of the order of the Knights Templar. Missing since the fourteenth century, the treasure is reputed to contain massive amounts of gold and silver bullion, the crown jewels of royal European families, religious artifacts sacred to both Judaism and Christianity, and documents that may be as explosive now as when they were buried. The estimated value of the potential treasure is more than one billion dollars.

Speaking

Work in small teams. Imagine that the government has 5 million dollars to support research for one of the mysteries from this unit. Choose the mystery that interests you the most and put together a good argument that includes the following:

- a description of the mystery;
- reasons why solving the mystery will help society; and
- an explanation of how you will study the mystery.

Make your argument in a formal presentation to a panel, which will decide who will receive the money.

Reading

Before You Read

Most countries have a secret intelligence service. Canada has Canadian Security Intelligence Service (CSIS), the US has the Central Intelligence Agency (CIA) and the United Kingdom has the Secret Intelligence Service, or MI6. In pairs, name your country's intelligence agency.

- What is the job of the agency?
- What is common knowledge about it? How secretive is the agency? How does it maintain its secrecy?
- What qualities and skills must a person have to work for the intelligence service?

Ninjas

1 **A** One of the deadliest secret societies that ever existed was "the invisible ones" – Japanese ninja warriors. During the sixteenth century, ninjas were highly feared assassins for hire. Powerful rulers of
5 regions fighting for control of Japan paid them to kill their enemies. Ninjas were not loyal to any individual ruler; they would murder whomever they were paid to kill.

B Ninjas spent long hours training to become
10 "invisible." One of the ninjas' main survival skills was using disguises. They needed to be able to move around like ordinary people during the day so they could learn about their victim and get close to him. Often they would dress as female musicians, danc-
15 ers, religious leaders, or merchants. This clothing allowed them to hide their true identity and weapons easily. Their skills let them move around without getting attention. They could move so silently that even guards had no idea they were there until it was too late
20 to save themselves or the person they were guarding.

C Ninjas were effective assassins because they could enter and leave without being seen. A ninja could slow his pulse and breathing and remain still for days while waiting for the person he wanted to kill. They could
25 also see in the dark. To do this they tried to keep the pupils in their eyes large by never looking directly at a light. This allowed them to move around easily at night. They were experts at the snoring patterns of both men and women and knew instantly when someone was fak-
30 ing sleep. Guards pretending to sleep were killed first. Ninjas killed anyone who got in the way.

D Ninjas were experts with several tools, but these needed to be small and light so they could move quickly and easily. One important ninja tool was poi-
35 son. The ninja hid in the ceiling and then lowered a thread to the sleeping victim's mouth. He would let poison run down the thread, killing the victim without ever leaving evidence he had been there. Ninjas used natural medicines from plants to heal their own
40 wounds and as poisons for their victims. They also

used *shuriken* (throwing stars), which were sharp, pointed flat disks made out of metal. They threw these disks to slow down any guards who chased them.

45   **E** To guard their secret ways, ninjas only taught the knowledge of their weapons and skills to their sons. Master ninjas also taught their students. If anyone was caught teaching their skills to the wrong people, they were killed. They kept their society 50 secret; consequently, everyone feared these invisible killers.

Freemasons

F One of the most well-known secret societies began in the late sixteenth or early seventeenth century in Scotland. During this time, many religious groups were 55 building large cathedrals and temples; princes and rich individuals were building castles. Many of these buildings took several years to finish. The construction of these great structures required workers with masonry skills because the buildings were made mostly from 60 stone. When the craftsmen started a new structure, the first thing they did was construct a building where they lived until the job was finished. Skilled workers from many countries, ethnic backgrounds, and religions worked together on these grand projects.

65   **G** The workers realized that they needed to make sure the projects could be completed easily. They created an organization of freemasons. Membership was not based on country, religion, or ethnicity; membership was based on having a skill needed in 70 the building process. While working on the projects, the craftsmen learned secret knowledge from the religious leaders, building designers, and well-educated individuals who they got to know. The freemasons also knew about the secret compartments 75 and tunnels in the buildings that they constructed. They organized the knowledge into different levels. Members could move up through the levels as they developed their professional skills and they could also learn secrets shared by other members at that

80 level. There were ceremonies, symbols, and rituals at each level.

H At that time, churches were very powerful and they did not like this non-religious group because it accepted people of all religions equally. The freemason 85 society became very secretive to protect its knowledge and survive. As it spread to other cities and countries, members needed ways to recognize fellow brothers, so they created a secret language of hand gestures, handshakes, and passwords to identify themselves as 90 genuine members of the freemason society.

Reading for Meaning

Find the underlined phrases in the paragraphs indicated and then choose the correct ending for each sentence.

1. <u>Highly feared assassins</u> are people who are *scared of being killed / scare others because they kill.* A

2. If the secret agent is <u>not loyal</u> to his country, he will *sell his country's secrets to the enemy / protect his country's secrets.* A

3. If you <u>move around</u>, you *walk in circles / travel.* B

4. If someone is <u>faking</u> illness, he is *acting to make you believe he is sick / trying to get better from an illness.* C

5. Telling the <u>wrong people</u> is the same as telling *people who make mistakes / people who should not know.* E

6. <u>Secret compartments</u> are *hidden spaces / hidden living areas.* G

7. If something has <u>spread to other cities</u>, it *has left one city to start again in another city / has stayed in one city and has also started in another city.* H

8. A <u>genuine</u> member is someone who *has been formally accepted by the group / wants to be a member of the group.* H

Reading for Similarities and Differences

Write the similarities and differences between the two secret societies.

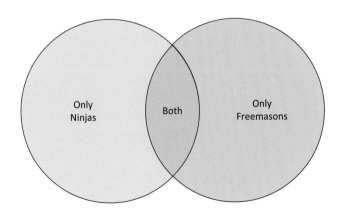

Thinking outside the Box

Complete the graphic organizer comparing one of the ancient secret societies and a modern day organization such as CSIS or a secret society of your choice.

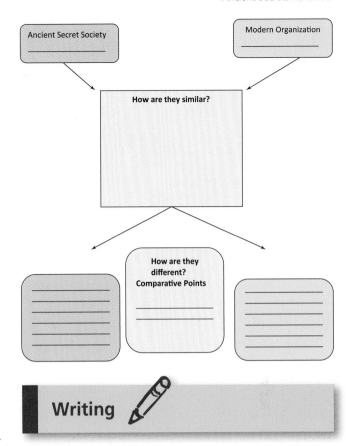

Writing

Use the information in your graphic organizer to write a paragraph comparing an old and a modern secret society.

Unit Reflection

Many people are willing to spend a lot of money and effort to understand the mysteries of the past. Why is this so important to people? How are ancient mysteries connected with our lives today?

Tic Tac Toe Answers

ritual: an action or ceremony that is usually repeated in the same pattern

secret: something that is not known by other people

forgery: a copy of something created to fool people

excavation: digging in an area of land to discover objects from the past

proof: a fact or piece of information which shows that something is true

mystery: something you cannot understand or explain

theory: an idea that tries to explain something

ancient: very old

reveal: make a secret known

Unit 3
O Canada, *Je t'aime*

Canada has a democratic government elected by the people. There are three levels of government: federal (Canada-wide), provincial (province-wide), and municipal (city-wide). The parliament buildings are in Ottawa, Ontario.

———————————————— ✦ ————————————————

There are three main groups of Aboriginal peoples in Canada: the First Nations, the Inuit, and the Métis. More than fifty different languages are spoken by Canada's Aboriginal peoples.

Canada was the first country to have a multicultural policy. It states that cultural and racial diversity are respected and supported, and that people are encouraged to keep their culture and language. Most Canadians are descendants of immigrants who came to Canada within the last 150 years. In 2006, there were 6.2 million foreign-born people from nearly two hundred countries living in Canada. They represented almost 20 percent of the total population. By 2031, nearly half (46 percent) of Canadians over the age of fifteen will have been born somewhere else in the world, or have at least one foreign-born parent.

Canada became a country on July 1, 1867. This event is known as "Confederation." Ontario, Quebec, Nova Scotia, and New Brunswick were the first colonies to unite the French and British systems and cultures into one unified country. The other provinces joined over the next eighty-two years. Confederation is celebrated on July 1—Canada Day.

More than 6.6 million Canadians speak French as their mother tongue. Most Francophones live in Quebec, but almost 1 million live in Canada's other provinces and territories. The areas with the smallest French-speaking populations are Prince Edward Island, Newfoundland and Labrador, and the three territories. The Official Languages Act (1969) states that all Canadians have the right to communicate with the federal government in English or French.

The government started the Canadian Broadcasting Corporation (CBC) to promote Canadian culture and a national identity. CBC Radio began in 1936, and television broadcasts began in 1952. CBC is distinctly Canadian. It reflects the diversity of the different regions and is broadcast in English and French. Radio programming is also broadcast in other languages, representing Canada's multiculturalism.

The Constitution is Canada's most important set of laws. In 1982, the Constitution was changed to give Canada full control of the country. Britain no longer had any responsibility for, or rule over, Canada. Quebec did not sign the Constitution in 1982 because the Quebecois wanted their language and culture to be recognized as distinct by law. In 1992, Canadians voted NO to accepting changes to the constitution to give Quebec unique recognition. To this day, Quebec has not signed the Constitution.

In three minutes list as many facts as you can about Canada not included on these pages.

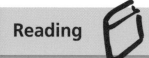

Reading

Before You Read

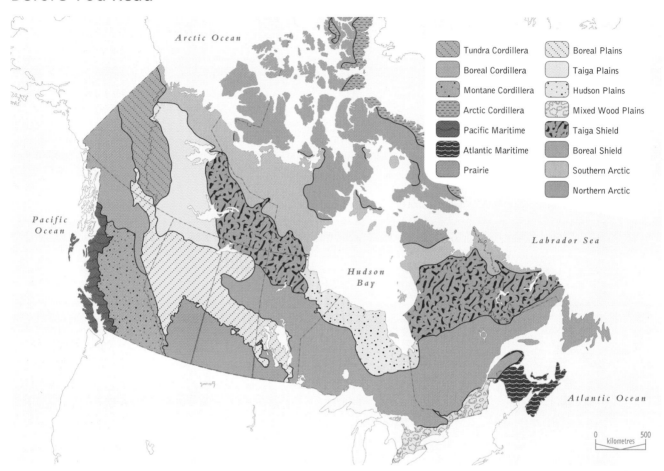

Using the geographical information on this land cover map, think about how you could divide Canada's ten provinces and three territories into five distinct regions.

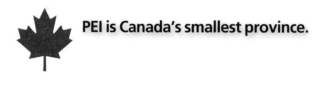

PEI is Canada's smallest province.

The North

1 **Snapshot:** Canada's northern region is made up of three territories: Nunavut, Yukon, and the Northwest Territories. The northern region covers over one third of Canada. It has a very small popu-
5 lation but a high Native population. Aboriginal languages are official languages along with English and French. Europeans first came to this area during the fur trades. Some people still make their living hunting and trapping in the North.

10 **Geology & Climate:** The southern region of the territories is in the lowlands. There are vast mountain ranges. Further north, beyond the tree line, is frozen tundra (the subsoil is frozen). The North is sometimes called "The Land of the Midnight Sun" because
15 in the summer, the daylight can last for twenty-four hours. During the brief summers the land blossoms. Winters in the North are long, cold, and dark. Yukon holds the record for the coldest temperature ever recorded in Canada, −63 degrees Celsius!

20 **Major Industries:** mining (zinc, gold, lead, diamonds), oil and gas exploration, tourism.

Pacific Coast

Snapshot: British Columbia, which borders the Pacific Ocean, is a nature lover's paradise. Sports lovers can kayak on the ocean and then drive high
25 into the mountains to go skiing the same day. The First Nations peoples were the first to inhabit the region. The best known examples of their art, which represents nature, are the totem poles that can be found throughout the province. Many descen-
30 dents of the Chinese workers who helped build the railroad and of early European settlers still live in British Columbia. BC is now home to many people from Asia and other parts of the world.

Geology & Climate: The climate is wet and
35 mild along the Pacific coast, and it often rains in Vancouver. Other parts of the province are much drier. Parts of BC are forested and mountainous.

Major Industries: tourism, mining, fishing, agriculture, forestry (BC produces half of Canada's lumber).

Newfoundland and Labrador was the last province to join Confederation, in 1949.

Nunavut became Canada's newest territory in 1999.

The Prairies

40 **Snapshot:** The Prairies are famous for their large stretches of flat land—the people who live there love the wide open spaces and blue sky. The First Nations people were the first to inhabit this area, where they skillfully hunted buffalo. The building of the railway
45 helped European settlers to move to the Prairies. Prairie farmers grow much of Canada's grain crops (wheat, oats, corn, etc.) and livestock (beef). Saskatchewan alone produces more than half of Canada's wheat. Alberta is also rich in natural resources such as oil
50 and natural gas. Each year, the Calgary Stampede tests and celebrates the skills of Canadian cowboys and entertains thousands of tourists. Tourists to Alberta also make sure they visit Dinosaur Provincial Park where they can see many dinosaur bones. Banff and
55 Jasper are two other famous parks known for their beautiful natural settings.

Geology & Climate: The Rocky Mountains border the Prairie provinces on the west. The flatlands border the Prairies on the east. The northern part
60 has countless rivers, lakes, forests, and bogs. The northern area also includes the Canadian Shield of Manitoba. This Shield is made up of some of the oldest rock on earth: it dates back to the last ice age. In southern Alberta, Chinook winds blow over the
65 Rocky Mountains. The warm dry winds can raise the temperature by 25 percent in a few hours.

Major Industries: agriculture (wheat, canola, livestock), forestry, mining (potash, uranium, coal, oil and natural gas, nickel, copper, zinc), manufacturing.

Central Canada

70 **Snapshot:** Ontario is Canada's second-largest province and has the most people. The Algonquin and Iroquois First Nations were the first inhabitants of the province. The population of Ontario grew rapidly starting in the 1700s. Many new immigrants
75 settle in Toronto, the capital city of Ontario, as well as in Ottawa, the capital city of Canada. Ontario's economy is very good due to its large population, rich resources, and location. Ontarians enjoy the great outdoors, participating in activities such as
80 swimming, hiking, fishing, tobogganing, skiing, skating, and snowmobiling.

Geology & Climate: There are three regions in Ontario: the Hudson Bay Lowlands, the Canadian Shield, and the Great Lakes–St. Lawrence Lowlands.
85 The climate in Southern Ontario is much warmer and less extreme than in Northern Ontario.

Major Industries: manufacturing, mining (gold, nickel, copper, uranium, zinc), forestry, financial industries, tourism.

90 **Snapshot:** The first inhabitants of Quebec were the First Nations peoples and the Inuit. In the 1600s, French settlers came to this area. This French heritage is uniquely reflected in Quebec society today. There has been an ongoing debate in Quebec 95 about separating from the rest of Canada. Many Quebecois feel this would better protect their language, religion, and heritage. Quebec City is the oldest city in Canada.

Geology & Climate: Most Quebecois live close 100 to the St. Lawrence River Valley. Mountain ranges separate the rich valleys from the rocky Canadian Shield, which covers most of Quebec. Quebec has three main climate regions. Southern and western Quebec have warm summers and long, cold win- 105 ters. Most of central Quebec has a subarctic climate.

Winters are long and cold, while summers are short and warm. The northern regions of Quebec have an arctic climate.

Major Industries: manufacturing, hydroelectric 110 generation, agriculture, mining (aluminum, iron ore), forestry.

The Atlantic Coast

Snapshot: Canada's Atlantic provinces include the three Maritime provinces (Prince Edward Island, New Brunswick, and Nova Scotia) and 115 Newfoundland and Labrador. The area was first inhabited by First Nations peoples who hunted and fished here for thousands of years. Hundreds of years ago, settlers from France, the British Isles, and Germany moved to this rugged coast. Some of 120 the earliest Black settlers and people escaping the American Revolutionary War moved to Nova Scotia

and New Brunswick. Tourists go to PEI to see the home of Anne of Green Gables. In New Brunswick, tourists visit Hopewell Cape to see the Flowerpot 125 Rocks exposed when the tide goes out. The famous Cabot Trail in Nova Scotia is a highway that hugs the coastline and reveals spectacular views of the ocean and steep hills, as well as the occasional whale. Visitors usually stop in Cape Breton to spend the 130 day at the Fortress of Louisbourg, a recreation of an eighteenth-century French fortress. Newfoundland is famous for its lighthouses and icebergs.

Geology & Climate: The maritime climate produces changing weather, with lots of precipitation 135 in many different forms. PEI is known for its rolling hills and natural beauty. Over 80 percent of New Brunswick is forested. Newfoundland is the easternmost part of Atlantic Canada and has a rugged ocean coast. Labrador is further north and is 140 mostly subarctic or arctic.

Major Industries: agriculture (potatoes, dairy), tourism, fishing, forestry, mining (coal, nickel, oil, natural gas), ship building.

Comprehension Check

All the statements below are false. Underline the sentences in the region profiles that prove this.

1. Most of New Brunswick is covered in good farmland.
2. Prairie farmers grow a small proportion of Canada's grain crops.
3. The climates in northern and southern Quebec are very similar.
4. No plant life can grow in northern Canada because it is too cold.
5. No relatives of the people who helped build the railway still live on the West Coast.
6. The northern part of Canada has daylight twenty-four hours a day in the winter.
7. The northern part of the Prairies is the Rocky Mountains.
8. The East Coast was first inhabited by the Germans.
9. The land along the West Coast is very dry and desertlike.
10. The climate in Northern Ontario is warmer than in Southern Ontario.

 Sir John A. Macdonald was the first prime minister of Canada. His picture is on the ten dollar bill.

Heading Completion

Complete the headings of each regional profile by adding the following provinces and territories.

Alberta, British Columbia, Manitoba, New Brunswick, Newfoundland and Labrador, Northwest Territories, Nova Scotia, Nunavut, Ontario, Prince Edward Island, Quebec, Saskatchewan, Yukon

Thinking outside the Box

Each of these famous Canadian artists has a strong connection to a particular region of Canada, which is evident in his or her art. Identify the regions that the artists' works represent.

a) Robert Bateman is a famous Canadian artist now living on Salt Spring Island in British Columbia. His paintings of Canada's wildlife are so realistic, they look like photographs.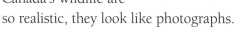

b) Lucy Maud Montgomery drew inspiration from the picturesque land of Prince Edward Island when she wrote her famous novel, *Anne of Green Gables*. This novel tells the story of Anne Shirley, an orphan, and the adventures she gets into. Thousands of tourists visit the home described in her novel every year.

c) W.O. Mitchell is a famous Canadian writer of novels, short stories, and plays. In 1947 he wrote the classic prairie novel *Who Has Seen the Wind*. This story describes the life of a young boy growing up in windy Saskatchewan, Mitchell's home province, during the Depression.

d) *Red Maple* is a painting by A.Y. Jackson, one of Canada's famous Group of Seven. These artists traveled mainly through the forests of Northern Ontario, painting landscapes of the beautiful rugged scenery in the 1920s.

e) Inuksuit are statues of stones that are used by the Inuit for communication and survival. The traditional meaning of the Inuksuk is "Someone was here" or "You are on the right path." They are still used as guides for navigating, markers for important places, and routes for good fishing. Artist Alvin Kanak of Rankin Inlet, Northwest Territories, created a famous Inuksuk.

f) Leonard Cohen is a singer/song-writer, musician, poet, and novelist born in Montreal. His work is recognized around the world. He has received the Companion of the Order of Canada, the nation's highest civilian honour. His famous song "Hallelujah" is a favourite of talent show contestants because of its great lyrics and melody.

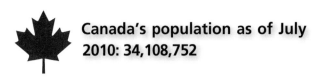

Canada's population as of July 2010: 34,108,752

Grammar Focus

Exercise A

In my opinion, Canada is **one of** the greatest <u>countries</u> in the world. It is a great place to live. Canada is large. In fact, Canada is the second largest country in the world, with 9,984,670 square kilometres of land. Almost **half of** <u>Canada</u> is covered in forests. It is a land of lakes and trees. The Great Lakes (Lake Superior, Lake Michigan, Lake Huron, Lake Erie, and Lake Ontario) are the largest group of fresh water lakes in the world. In fact, nearly **one-fourth of** the fresh <u>water</u> in the world is in Canada. There are **many** provincial and national <u>parks</u> across Canada. In the summer, camping, hiking, biking, swimming, and fishing are a few of the <u>sports</u> that people enjoy. In the winter, snowmobiling, skiing, skating, hockey, and snowboarding are popular.

There are ten provinces and three territories. **Each** province and territory has a capital city. **Every** <u>province and territory</u> also has its own government. **Much of** <u>Canada</u> is sparsely populated. Most <u>Canadians</u> (75 percent) live within 160 kilometres of the Canada–United States border. **Some of** the provinces border oceans. **Several** <u>provinces,</u> such as Ontario, Manitoba, Saskatchewan, and Alberta, do not. Canada is a vast country of great beauty stretching from the Pacific Ocean to the Atlantic Ocean. The Trans-Canada Highway is one of the largest national roads in the world (7821 kilometres)—it stretches from Victoria, BC, to St. John's, Newfoundland.

- Look at the words or phrases in bold. What kind of information do they give about the words that follow?
- Look at the underlined words or phrases. What is the function of these words in the sentence?

1. What parts of speech are the bolded words?
2. List the bolded words that modify singular countable nouns.
3. List the bolded words that modify plural countable nouns.
4. List the bolded words that modify uncountable nouns.
5. List the bolded phrases that are followed by articles.

A quantifier is a word or phrase that comes before a noun and describes *how many* or *how much*. Which quantifier to use depends on whether the noun that follows is countable or uncountable.

Exercise B

Write the bolded expression that has the same meaning as the following:

1. a single: _____
2. a small number of: _____
3. a large amount of: _____
4. 25 percent of: _____
5. a large number: _____
6. almost all: _____
7. emphasizes one member of many in a group: _____
8. 50 percent of: _____
9. emphasizes a common fact among all members of a group: _____

Quantifiers of SINGULAR COUNTABLE NOUNS	Quantifiers of PLURAL COUNTABLE NOUNS	Quantifiers of UNCOUNTABLE NOUNS
Refer to Appendix p. 146 for meanings of the words.		
any	any	(a) little
each	both	less
every	(a) few	much
numerals	many	all
either	several	most
neither	half	more
	all	some
	most	
	more	
	some	

Note: **lots of** and **a lot of** are common quantifiers used with plural countable nouns or uncountable nouns.

Exercise C

Complete each sentence with one of the following quantifiers: **much, many, few, little, most**

1. Mining is a major industry in _____ provinces.
2. There is _____ chance that polar bears will wander far from the frozen arctic.
3. Canadians spend _____ time enjoying the great outdoors.
4. In _____ areas of Canada there are four distinctive seasons.
5. Gardeners have _____ success growing tropical plants in Ontario.
6. _____ Canadians live in the territories.
7. The Prairies do not get _____ rain.
8. There are _____ natural resources in PEI.
9. _____ young Canadians play hockey and dream of being on an NHL team.
10. _____ Canadians can speak some French because they studied it in elementary school.

Few and **little** have the same grammatical function as **a few** and **a little**, but their meanings are different. **Few** and **little** indicate that there is not enough of something or it is not easy to get. **A few** and **a little** mean a small amount. Complete the sentences with one of the following quantifiers: **a few, few, little, a little**

11. _____ people live in northern Canada.
12. For _____ energy burst, I like to eat maple sugar candies.
13. There is _____ rainfall in the dry Prairie provinces.

14. _____ people ever travel to the North Pole.
15. _____ species of bears live in Canada.
16. _____ plant life grows in the frozen tundra.
17. I would like to try _____ piece of that pie, please.
18. Every year there are _____ snowstorms on the East Coast that close the Trans-Canada Highway.

> - If you want to point out that the quantifying phrase refers to a single member or part of a specific and identifiable group, use the phrase *of the* after the qualifier. Omit *the* if the noun being modified is a proper noun.
> - If the quantifier precedes articles (a/an/the), demonstratives (this/that/these/those), or possessive determiners (my/your/our), it is always followed by *of*.
> - The verb agrees in number with the noun that follows the quantifier.
>
> Note: *one*, *each*, and *every* normally take singular verbs, whether or not they are followed by *of*.

Exercise D

Complete each sentence with the correct form of the verb in parentheses.

1. All of the forests _____ deciduous. (be)
2. Some of the provinces _____ on the coast. (be)
3. Half of the resources _____ not renewable. (be)
4. Many of the people _____ close to the US border. (live)
5. Much of the water _____ fresh water. (be)
6. Twenty percent of the forest _____ going to be cut down. (be)
7. Much of New Brunswick _____ covered in trees. (be)
8. Several of the provinces _____ on the Canadian Shield. (be)
9. One of the provinces _____ on the West Coast. (be)
10. A couple of the provinces _____ in the Central region. (be)

Pronunciation Power

Joining words together is known as linking. Linking helps to make English speech sound smooth.

When one word ends with a consonant sound and the next word begins with a vowel sound, the final consonant sound of the first word is linked to the vowel sound at the beginning of the next word.

Example: great deal of /diːl/ + /əv/

Exercise A

Draw arrows to indicate the linking in Grammar Focus, Exercise D. Listen to check your answers. Practise reading the sentences with a partner.

Exercise B

Listen to the ten sentences and circle the quantifier or quantifier phrase that you hear.

1. all / all of the
2. most / most of the
3. some / some of the
4. each / each of the
5. several / several of the
6. both / both of the
7. half / half of the
8. each / each of the
9. few / few of the
10. several / several of the

Exercise C

Write the sentences that you hear. Underline the quantifier.

1. _____
2. _____
3. _____
4. _____
5. _____
6. _____

Grammar in Use

Work with a partner. Make a True/False quiz about Canada, using statements with quantifiers. Exchange your quiz with another pair.

Example:

T/F   Most of the wheat in Canada is grown in Saskatchewan.

T/F   Most people live within two hundred kilo-metres of the northern border of Canada.

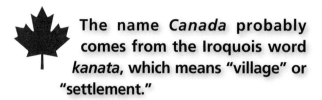

The name *Canada* probably comes from the Iroquois word *kanata,* which means "village" or "settlement."

Video

Vocabulary

Exercise A

Complete the sentences describing regions of Canada with the following words:

arctic	Maritime	region
borders	mountain	territories
coast	natural	tundra
climate	resources	valleys
forests	Prairie	
landscapes	provinces	

a) There are vast 1 _____ ranges and further north, beyond the tree line, is frozen 2 _____ (subsoil is frozen).

b) 3 _____ farmers grow much of Canada's grain crops.

c) The Rocky Mountains border the Prairie 4 _____ on the west.

d) British Columbia, which 5 _____ the Pacific Ocean, is a nature lover's paradise.

e) The southern 6 _____ of the 7 _____ are in the lowlands.

f) Alberta is also rich in 8 _____ such as oil and natural gas.

g) These artists travelled mainly through the 9 _____ of Northern Ontario, painting 10 _____ .

h) Mountain ranges separate the rich 11 _____ from the rocky Canadian Shield, which covers most of Quebec.

i) The northern regions of Quebec have an 12 _____ climate.

j) Newfoundland is the easternmost part of Atlantic Canada and has a rugged ocean 13 _____.

k) Canada's Atlantic provinces include the three 14 _____ provinces.

l) Quebec has three main 15 _____ regions.

Exercise B

Match the following definitions to the word choices in Exercise A

a) _____: a large northern area where trees do not grow and the ground is frozen

b) _____: a large area of flat land without trees

c) _____: general weather conditions for an area

d) _____: a very large hill

e) _____: the land that borders the sea

f) _____: the line that separates two areas

g) _____: a land area that is distinct from other land areas

h) _____: area within Canada that has a separate government

i) _____: large areas of land within Canada that have small populations and a separate government

j) _____: materials that come from the land

k) _____: a view of the natural environment of an area

l) _____: low area of land between two higher areas

m) _____: extremely cold

n) _____: relating to the sea

o) _____: large area of land covered in trees growing close together

Exercise C

Give examples of the following from world geography:

mountain

coast

border

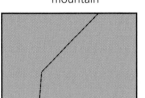
forest

province

maritime

valley

LANDSCAPE

TUNDRA

The Quebec City Winter Carnival is the largest winter festival in the world.

Province/Territory	Postal Symbol
Alberta	AB
British Columbia	BC
Manitoba	MB
New Brunswick	NB
Newfoundland and Labrador	NL
Northwest Territories	NT
Nova Scotia	NS
Nunavut	NU
Ontario	ON
Prince Edward Island	PE
Quebec	QC
Saskatchewan	SK
Yukon*	YT

*Effective 1 April 2003, the name of the territory became Yukon, as per the Yukon Act (C. 7 SC 27 March, 2002). A new postal symbol and a new abbreviation have not been determined.

Exercise D

Complete the word webs by listing words you associate with the word in the box.

ARCTIC

NATURAL RESOURCES

The Vikings may have been the first Europeans to arrive in North America. They reached the East Coast in 986 CE.

Vocabulary in Use

Using the vocabulary words in Exercise A, label or draw images on the map.

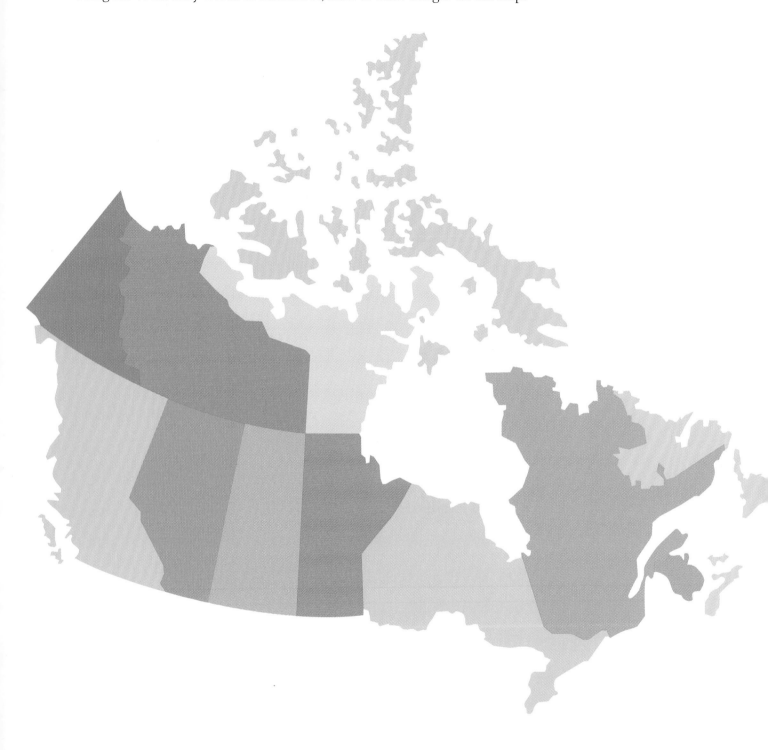

Speaking

Work in groups of two to six players divided into two teams. You need a die and two markers.

1. Place your markers on the START square. Roll the die – highest number goes first. Move your marker the number of spaces indicated on the die.
2. Each square has the name of a region in Canada and a symbol.

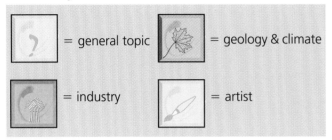

? = general topic

🍁 = geology & climate

🌾 = industry

🖌 = artist

3. When you land on a square, make two statements about the topic indicated by the symbol for that region. For example, if you land on 🖌, make two statements about an artist from the Atlantic region. If the opposing team agrees with your statements, remain on the square. Then, the opposing team takes its turn. If your statements are incorrect, return to the square you moved from. The opposing team takes its turn.
4. The team to reach the finish first wins.

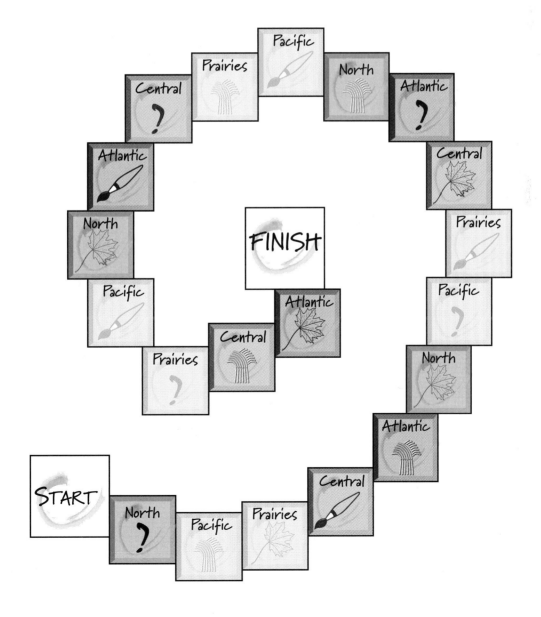

Listening

Before You Listen

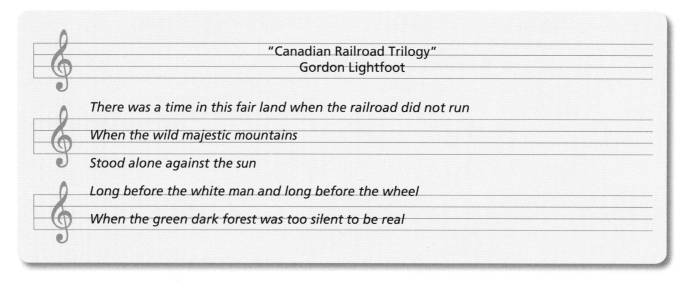

"Canadian Railroad Trilogy"
Gordon Lightfoot

There was a time in this fair land when the railroad did not run

When the wild majestic mountains

Stood alone against the sun

Long before the white man and long before the wheel

When the green dark forest was too silent to be real

Look at the first stanza of the song.

1. To what time in history does this refer?
2. What region of Canada is it about?
3. What do you think the song will be about?

Listening for Specific Information

Listen to the following brief history of the building of Canada's railroad to answer the following questions:

1. How did the railroad help Canada become a country?
2. What made building the railroad dangerous work?
3. How long did it take to build the railroad?

Listening for Meaning

Listen to the song in segments. Circle the letter of the phrases that best describe the message the songwriter is trying to tell.

Segment 1: a) the importance of the forest and mountains
b) a description of the land before the railroad
c) the influence of the white man living in the forest

Segment 2: a) workers from other countries came to build the railway and some gambled their money away
b) Canadian workers built the railway and some lost or won a lot of money

c) men walked around the country and gambled in the spring

Segment 3: a) the sea connects the east and west
b) the railroad connects the east to the west
c) the shipping ports connect the east to the west

Segment 4: a) work on the railway caused a lot of injuries
b) the workers believed with all their heart that the railway would be good for the country
c) workers are needed to dig up the land to lay the railway tracks quickly

Segment 5: a) it's a hard life and the workers missed their families
b) workers in the navy worked long hours
c) workers worked long hours and then ate and drank with their loved ones

Segment 6: a) they fought on the mountaintops
b) they cried when they finished
c) they completed the railroad

Segment 7 (last line): a) many men died building the railroad
b) many men died before the white man came
c) men died after the railroad was built

Listening to Retell

How would you describe this song to a friend? Complete this statement: This is a song about….

Thinking outside the Box

Create a story describing the life of one of the workers who helped build the railway. Include the following:

- the worker's name;
- the reason for coming to Canada;
- the worker's life back home;
- the type of work he did;
- the risks involved with his work;
- his living conditions;
- his daily routine; and
- how he felt about his experience in Canada.

Writing

Working in small groups, create a travel brochure for one of the regions of Canada. Include the following information:

- a message that attracts tourists to the area;
- sports or activities you can do there;
- two popular tourist attractions;
- a description of the people who live there; and
- the provinces or territories, the capitals, and the official flags and flowers.

Select the best brochure for the class.

Unit Reflection

Complete the following sentences based on what you have learned in this unit.

Canada is a country that. . . .

Canada has. . . .

I didn't know that. . . .

I'm surprised that. . . .

I already knew that. . . .

The most interesting thing about Canada to me is. . . .

Lacrosse is the national summer sport of Canada. The Aboriginal people of Canada invented the game of lacrosse.

Hockey is the national winter sport of Canada.

UNITED STATES

Perhaps the most shocking find: Americans goof off on the Web slightly less than the global average.

19	10.2	8.8	5.7
TV	RADIO	INTERNET	READING

CANADA

Come on, Canadians. Isn't there anything good on TV up there?

14.7	9.1	8.3	5.8
TV	RADIO	INTERNET	READING

UNITED KINGDOM

People in the UK spend more than three times as many hours watching TV as they do reading.

TV	RADIO	INTERNET	READING

SPAIN

The Spanish don't watch much TV, relatively speaking, but they sure like the Internet.

15.9	9.9	11.5	5.8
TV	RADIO	INTERNET	READING

ITALY

Italy ranks near the bottom for all leisure-time activities. Italians must be too busy enjoying their spaghetti and meatballs to spend their free time any other way.

14.9	7.2	6.3	5.6
TV	RADIO	INTERNET	READING

MEXICO

Mexicans watch less TV than anyone; but with all that sun, wouldn't you also rather be listening to the radio at the beach?

TV	RADIO	INTERNET	READING

BRAZIL

When it comes to relaxation, Brazilians prefer electronics over books.

18.4	17.2	10.5	5.2
TV	RADIO	INTERNET	READING

ARGENTINA

This is a DJ's paradise: Argentina is one of the few places where people listen to the radio more than they watch TV.

14	20.8	8.9	5.9
TV	RADIO	INTERNET	READING

Leisure Time around the World

DISCUSSION

1. Data is information collected for research. Read the description for those countries where the data is missing. Match the data sets below to the appropriate countries.

a)

18	10.5	8.8	5.3
TV	RADIO	INTERNET	READING

b)

11.6	11.1	6.3	5.5
TV	RADIO	INTERNET	READING

c)

15.7	2.1	10.8	8
TV	RADIO	INTERNET	READING

d)

17.3	9	8.8	6.9
TV	RADIO	INTERNET	READING

2. What conclusions can you make?

   - Compare the Canadian and US data.

   - In order to make appropriate conclusions, we need to ask questions about what the data actually describe. What additional questions could you ask to help understand the data? For example, according to the study, reading is the least favourite leisure activity worldwide. Does reading include reading on the Internet?

3. If included here, how do your home country's leisure activities compare to the Canadian data? What might explain the similarities or differences?

SWEDEN
Swedes were among the most well-rounded time-wasters of those polled.

12.3	10.9	8	6.9
TV	RADIO	INTERNET	READING

FRANCE
Although about average in most categories, the French spend nearly twice as many hours watching TV as doing anything else with their leisure time

TV	RADIO	INTERNET	READING

RUSSIA
Rebuilding a country doesn't leave much time for relaxation.

15	6.6	8.9	7.1
TV	RADIO	INTERNET	READING

TURKEY
People in Turkey spend a lot of time doing everything except reading.

20.2	13.3	10.6	5.9
TV	RADIO	INTERNET	READING

JAPAN
The Japanese manage to watch an above-average amount of TV, but they seem to be too busy for everything else.

17.9	4.1	6.9	4.1
TV	RADIO	INTERNET	READING

SAUDI ARABIA
Saudis have tuned out when it comes to listening to the radio.

17.7	3.9	9.3	6.8
TV	RADIO	INTERNET	READING

SOUTH KOREA
South Koreans have the distinction of reading less than any country polled. Judging by the numbers, they must be within range of a lot of Chinese radio stations, too.

15.4	3	9.6	3.1
TV	RADIO	INTERNET	READING

EGYPT
Please tell us they aren't spending all of those hours watching *Friends* reruns.

20.9	9	10.3	7.5
TV	RADIO	INTERNET	READING

INDIA
Read a good book lately? If you live in India, the answer is most likely "yes."

13.3	4.1	7.9	10.7
TV	RADIO	INTERNET	READING

CHINA
Chinese radio stations must really stink, but apparently the Chinese console themselves with computers and books.

TV	RADIO	INTERNET	READING

THAILAND
Thailand's media use ranked near the top in all four categories.

22.4	13.3	11.7	9.4
TV	RADIO	INTERNET	READING

SOUTH AFRICA
South Africans divide their leisure time almost equally between the TV and the radio.

14.8	15	9	6.3
TV	RADIO	INTERNET	READING

AUSTRALIA
Forget about the TV: surf's up.

13.3	11.3	7	6.3
TV	RADIO	INTERNET	READING

All averages are measured in hours per week, and Internet averages don't include time spent using this medium at work.

Speaking

In small groups, create a question for each of the following topics and survey the class. Decide what kind of information you will collect about each topic. Graph the data you collect and present it to the rest of the class.

 surfing the Internet

 listening to music

 watching movies

 reading

 watching TV

How many hours of TV do you watch every week?

What is your favourite TV program?

Do you watch more, less, or the same amount of TV as you did five years ago?

Do you think the quality of TV programs is better, worse, or the same as it was five years ago?

Reading

The Nielsen Company is the world's leading media and information company. It collects information from people about their opinions and habits. The information in the reading is taken from a recent research report on teen media trends. The Nielsen Company does research in more than a hundred countries.

Before You Read

Test your knowledge about youth media trends around the world. Work with a partner to complete the quiz. Circle true (*T*) or false (*F*) for each statement.

T F 1. Young people are spending less time watching television and more time on the Internet.

T F 2. American youth watch more television than any other country's youth.

T F 3. Teens spend more time on computers and the Internet than any other age group.

T F 4. China's youth spend more time on the Internet than any other country's youth.

T F 5. The most popular mobile phone activity is downloading ringtones.

T F 6. American youth use the Internet on their mobile phones more than any other teens.

T F 7. Globally, teens use handheld video game systems more than console game systems.

T F 8. In the US, girls spend just as much time playing console games as boys.

Jigsaw Reading

Divide into four teams. All teams will read the introduction and ONE assigned section, and complete the questions that follow. After your team has completed the reading, form a new team with one person from each of the other groups. Tell your teammates about the research you read and give the correct answers to the Before You Read quiz questions for your section of the reading.

How Teens Use Media

It's easy to believe the hype about teenagers promoted in the media. The idea that teens are too busy texting and Twittering to use traditional media like radio and television is exciting, but false. Teens are unique, but they are not as out-of-the-ordinary as some people might think. It is true that they are extremely comfortable using digital media. After all, they have grown up with digital technology. They communicate with each other all the time using technology and they do work on several different tasks at the same time. However, they are also still TV viewers, newspaper readers and radio listeners even if some people think they are not. Studies have shown that teens accept new media quickly, but they do not give up traditional media because of this. They use new media in addition to traditional media. Overall, the media habits of teens are not very different from the media habits of the total population.

This report provides evidence that some popular beliefs about how teens use media are wrong. It shows the reality about how teens use media.

TV Makes the World Go Round

Myth: Teens are giving up TV for new media.

Reality: Wrong. In fact, they watch more TV than ever, up 6 percent over the past five years in the US. Television is still the most popular medium for teenagers.

Myth: American teens watch more TV than anyone else.

Reality: Far from true . . . South Africans and Indonesians watch much more TV than American teens.

Compared to teens in other countries, US teens actually watch less television per day than most. In South Africa, teens averaged more than five hours per day of TV viewing. In Taiwan, teens averaged just two hours and forty-seven minutes. In terms of types of programs, reality or participation/variety programs appeal to teenagers across the markets measured, while sports and information (news) are almost never included among the three best liked genres. Globally, drama, in the form of general drama, soap operas, and telenovelas, tends to be more popular with teen viewers than comedy.

---

medium: the singular form of the word media. Media refers to the ways people get information. It includes television, radio, newspapers, magazines, Internet, and computers as a group.

genre: a style, especially in art

appeal: are interesting to

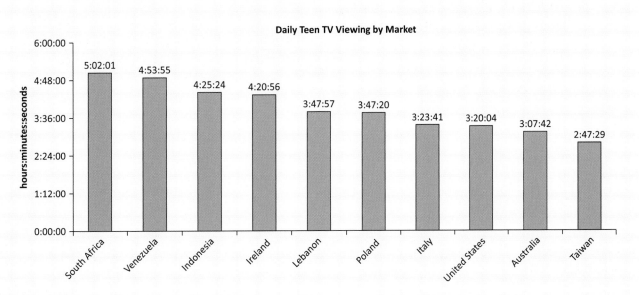

Daily Teen TV Viewing by Market

hours:minutes:seconds

South Africa	5:02:01
Venezuela	4:53:55
Indonesia	4:25:24
Ireland	4:20:56
Lebanon	3:47:57
Poland	3:47:20
Italy	3:23:41
United States	3:20:04
Australia	3:07:42
Taiwan	2:47:29

Comprehension Check

1. What information supports your T/F choices for 1 and 2 in the Before You Read quiz?
2. What is the most appealing genre of TV program, according to this reading?

Reading a Graph

What do you notice when comparing television viewing in Poland and Lebanon; Italy and the US; and Ireland and Indonesia?

The Internet Generation

Myth: Teens are the most popular users of the Internet.

Reality: Teens browse the Internet less than half as much as the typical user.

Many people think of today's teens as the Internet generation: Born in the 1990s, today's teens grew up with a computer mouse in their hands. They are very comfortable with digital technology and they are always connected to other people and information. In fact, approximately 90 percent of US teens have access to the Internet at home and 73 percent have access on a school PC. Among teens with Internet access at home, 55 percent say they have a wireless connection.

Even with this high degree of access and excellent knowledge of computers, teens actually spend less time on computers and the Internet than other age groups. As a recent Nielsen report[1] revealed, the typical US teenager spends eleven hours and thirty-two minutes a month on the Web, less than half the US average of twenty-nine hours and fifteen minutes per month for all ages surveyed.

Internet access: a connection to the Internet

[1]Nielsen's Q1 2009 Three Screen Report

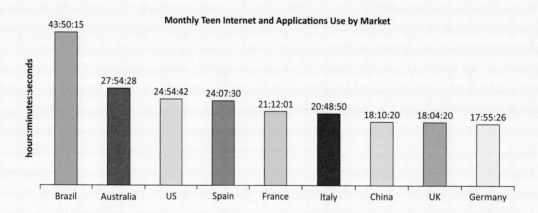

Monthly Teen Internet and Applications Use by Market

hours:minutes:seconds

Brazil	Australia	US	Spain	France	Italy	China	UK	Germany
43:50:15	27:54:28	24:54:42	24:07:30	21:12:01	20:48:50	18:10:20	18:04:20	17:55:26

Comprehension Check

1. What information supports your T/F choices for 3 and 4 in the Before You Read quiz?
2. How common is wireless access at home for American teens?

Reading a Graph

In which two countries do teens spend the most time on the Internet? What do you notice about the number of hours spent online in the top-ranking country, the second-ranking country, and all other countries?

Mobile: Always Connected

Myth: The only way to communicate with teens over the phone is by texting.

Reality: Teens do text a lot, but they are quick to accept all mobile media.

Of all the mobile activities of teens, texting is most talked about. Eighty-three percent of US teens with cellphones use text messaging and 56 percent use MMS/picture messaging. The average US teen now sends or receives an average of 2,899 text messages per month compared to 191 calls. The average number of texts has gone up 566 percent in just two years. There has been almost no increase in the average number of calls during that time.

Still, texting isn't the only way to communicate with teens over the mobile phone. Teens use many advanced mobile data features. More than a third of teens download ringtones, instant message, or use the mobile Web, while about a quarter of US teens download games and applications.

There is a popular belief that teens in the US may be far behind users in other markets who access the Internet on their cellphones. In fact, US teens accept and become comfortable using mobile media more quickly than in many of the markets Nielsen studies. Consider mobile Web: as of Q1 2009, 37 percent of US paying users of mobile phones, thirteen to seventeen, accessed the Internet on their phone—this puts US teens in second position behind 50 percent of China's teens with mobile devices.

---

average: in mathematics: add individual numbers and divide by the number of individual items (e.g., (a + b + c) ÷ 3 = average)

market: business of buying and selling

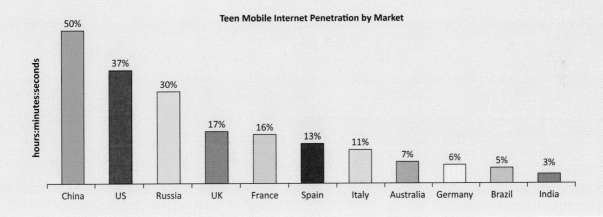

Teen Mobile Internet Penetration by Market

y-axis: hours:minutes::seconds

China 50% | US 37% | Russia 30% | UK 17% | France 16% | Spain 13% | Italy 11% | Australia 7% | Germany 6% | Brazil 5% | India 3%

Comprehension Check

1. What information supports your T/F choices for 5 and 6 in the Before You Read quiz?
2. How did the increase in the number of text messages compare with the increase in the number of telephone calls during a recent two-year period?

Reading a Graph

The chart shows the percentage of teen mobile subscribers in different countries who access the Internet on their mobile phone. Which country's teens rank eighth?

Gaming

Myth: Teens are the biggest gamers of all.

Reality: Only 23 percent of the console audience are teens and less than 10 percent of PC game minutes are played by teens.

When we think of teen media use, gaming is often one of the first activities we consider. Over the past twenty years, though, the gaming audience has grown to include new groups of users. New devices and games have made gaming more popular with girls, and—with the introduction of Nintendo's Wii—children and older people, too. Console, PC, and handheld gaming still plays an important role in the media lives of teens, though.

The typical US teen used a video game console an average of twenty-five minutes per day in 2008, for gaming or other multimedia uses—an average that has increased over the past five years as video game consoles have become better. The average daily console use is much higher for teen boys (forty-one minutes) than for teen girls (eight minutes).

Handheld video game systems are also popular with teens, particularly in the US Globally, 30 percent of teens have access to a console video game system.

---

console game: a video game machine that is connected to a TV screen
PC game: a video game played on a personal computer
devices: machines
handheld video game systems: small gaming machines that you can carry around with you

---

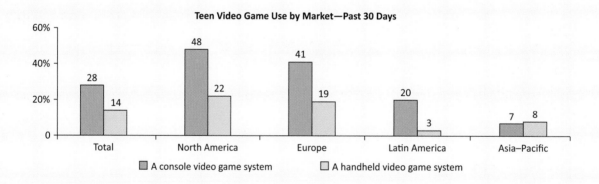

Teen Video Game Use by Market—Past 30 Days

- A console video game system
- A handheld video game system

Comprehension Check

1. What information supports your T/F choices for 7 and 8 in the Before You Read quiz?
2. Why has time spent playing console games in the US increased in the last five years?

Reading a Graph

The chart compares console game use and handheld game use in different areas of the world. What do you notice about the relationship between console and handheld game use in most of the world?

Thinking outside the Box

Data is information about a topic in the form of facts and numbers. An *analysis* is a detailed study of data in order to discover more about a particular topic. This Nielsen report gives facts about teen media use, but it does not give reasons to explain the data.

The following statements are true according to the Nielsen report. In small groups, brainstorm possible reasons for the data. Of course, we cannot be certain of the reasons without more research.

1. Television is still the most popular medium for teenagers.

2. In terms of type, reality or participation/variety programs appeal to teenagers across the markets.

3. Teens actually spend less time on computers and the Internet than the general population.

4. The average number of texts has gone up 566 percent in just two years, yet there has been almost no increase in the average number of calls during that time.

5. In the US, the average daily console use is much higher for teen boys (forty-one minutes) than for teen girls (eight minutes).

SNAPSHOT OF CANADA

According to a recent research study comparing the impact of Internet use in twelve countries,
- one-third of Canadian kids have parents as a contact on their social-networking profile;
- 68 percent of online parents in Canada report the Internet has improved their relationship with their family; and
- of the twelve countries surveyed, parents in Canada are most likely to say they are extremely or very knowledgeable in discussing Internet activities in which their children have been involved.

Writing

The data below are from a survey that shows similarities and differences about online youth in twelve countries and five continents. Look at the chart. In small groups, discuss the data. Choose two or three interesting points and write a short report-style paragraph to explain the information. Use the style in the reading section as a model. The paragraph has been started for you.

Useful vocabulary:

twice (three times, four times...) as much/many

to estimate

Online Youth around the World

Children around the world report spending more time online than their parents think they do. On average across the twelve countries, children say they spend…

Different Perspectives

How many hours per month do you spend on the Internet?
Base: Youth *n*=2614; Parents *n*=1297

Country	Actual Number of Hours Kids Spend Online	Number of Hours Parents Think Kids Spend Online	Difference
Total	39 (*n*=2614)	21 (*n*=1297)	+18
UK	44 (*n*=238)	19 (*n*=112)	+25
US	42 (*n*=220)	18 (*n*=100)	+24
Australia	49 (*n*=227)	28 (*n*=108)	+21
France	42 (*n*=203)	23 (*n*=151)	+19
Japan	31 (*n*=211)	13 (*n*=108)	+18
Germany	34 (*n*=208)	20 (*n*=102)	+14
Brazil	70 (*n*=204)	56 (*n*=100)	+14
India	34 (*n*=206)	21 (*n*=101)	+13
Sweden	59 (*n*=216)	46 (*n*=105)	+13
Italy	40 (*n*=214)	27 (*n*=107)	+13
Canada	42 (*n*=206)	30 (*n*=103)	+12
China	33 (*n*=261)	21 (*n*=100)	+12

Pronunciation Power

When we talk about research, it's important to pronounce numbers and express relationships clearly.

Exercise A

Two important parts of pronunciation are syllables and word stress. Listen to the measurement expressions. Draw a line to separate the syllables, and mark the main stress.

Example: percent – per/cènt

Measurement Expressions

%	percent
<	less than	+ non-countable noun
		(less than 10 percent of information)
	fewer than	+ countable noun
		(fewer than 10 percent of people)
>	more than
~	approximately
¼	one-fourth
	one-quarter
½	one-half
⅓	one-third
¾	three-quarters

Exercise B

1. Listen to each number pair. What do you notice about the sound the letter *t* makes in each word in the pair?

Numbers

a) thirteen (13)
   thirty (30)

b) fourteen (14)
   forty (40)

c) fifteen (15)
   fifty (50)

d) sixteen (16)
   sixty (60)

e) seventeen (17)
   seventy (70)

f) eighteen (18)
   eighty (80)

g) nineteen (19)
   ninety (90)

The letter *t* in numbers that end in teen is pronounced differently than the *t* in numbers that end in *–ty*. In numbers ending in *teen* the *t* is pronounced /t/. In numbers ending in *–ty* the *t* is pronounced /d/. Also, it is important to pronounce the final /n/ sound in *teen* so the number is not mistaken for a number that ends in *–ty*.

2. It's important to say the ending consonant sounds in numbers clearly. Listen to the sentences and write the number you hear in the blanks. Practise saying the sentences with a partner.

a) _____ percent of participants said they watched movies online.

b) _____ percent of participants said they watched movies online.

c) Participants said they spent less than _____ hours per week browsing the Web.

d) Participants said they spent less than _____ hours per week browsing the Web.

e) _____ percent of gamers bought a game in the last month.

f) _____ percent of gamers bought a game in the last month.

g) Most cellphone users received more than _____ text messages per day.

h) Most cellphone users received more than _____ text messages per day.

i) The number of people listening to this radio program has decreased by _____ percent.

j) The number of people listening to this radio program has decreased by _____ percent.

k) Advertising sales for the newspaper have decreased by _____ percent.

l) Advertising sales for the newspaper have decreased by _____ percent.

m) More than _____ specialty TV channels were added in the last year.

n) More than _____ specialty TV channels were added in the last year.

Exercise C

Information is missing. In small groups, discuss what the graph will describe. Then, listen to the information to complete the graph. Write the correct numbers at the top of each bar graph. The total has been done for you.

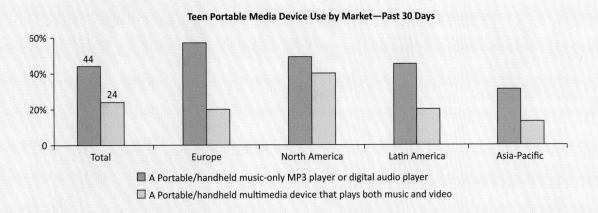

Teen Portable Media Device Use by Market—Past 30 Days

■ A Portable/handheld music-only MP3 player or digital audio player
□ A Portable/handheld multimedia device that plays both music and video

Exercise D

Work with a partner. Partner A should look at the sentences on page 158 in the Appendix while Partner B works with this page. Partner A will choose one of the sentences in each pair and read it aloud. Partner B will circle which information he or she hears. Check the answers. Then, Partner B should look at the sentences on page 143 in the Appendix while Partner A works with this page.

Partner A	Partner B

1. a) 6 or 7%
   b) 67%
	6. a) More than 3/4
	   b) More than 1/4

2. a) 12 to 70
   b) 12 to 17
	7. a) 92%
	   b) 90%

3. a) 57%
   b) 5 to 7%
	8. a) Nearly 16% . . . 41
	   b) Nearly 60% . . . 41

4. a) More than 2/3 . . . about 3/4
   b) More than 1/3 . . . about 1/4
	9. a) 40% . . . in India (37%) and Brazil (25%)
	   b) 14% . . . in India (47%) and Brazil (25%)

5. a) 45% . . . 4 or more
   b) 45% . . . 3 or 4
	10. a) 1/3
	    b) 2/3

Now, with your partner, read all the sentences aloud again and decide which sentence in each pair you think is true.

Grammar Focus

I read this cartoon about blogging yesterday. It was a conversation between a man and a dog. The man said that he didn't have anything to write about in his blog. When the dog suggested that the man write about what he had for lunch, the man said that he had already put a photo of his lunch on Facebook. I thought that was funny.

Compare the statements the woman makes on the phone with the statements the man makes in the cartoon. What is the woman doing when she makes her statements?

Exercise A

1. Circle the sentences that report statements made by others.
    a) The superstar couple announced that they were ending their three-year marriage.
    b) The superstar couple's three-year marriage has ended.
    c) British actor Michael Fellows was not drunk at the time of the accident.
    d) British actor Michael Fellows admitted that he was drunk at the time of the accident.
    e) The company will release a new version of the game next month.
    f) The company said that it would release its new version of the game next year.
    g) Users of the popular social = networking site said that they were happy with the company's design changes.
    h) Executives at the popular social = networking site said that users were happy with its design changes.
    i) Film critics across the country love this movie.
    j) Film critics across the country hate this movie.

Exercise B

Compare the statements in the cartoon with the woman's phone conversation.

*   What do you notice about how reported sentences begin?
*   What two grammatical changes do you notice in the reported sentences?

Reporting Statements

It is common to be in a situation where we report what another person has said. We might report what someone has said in a conversation, a spoken or written interview, or a research study.

Introducing the Reported Clause

When we report what another person has said, we introduce the reported speech with (1) the noun or pronoun that shows who made the original statement and (2) a reporting verb such as *said, asked*, or *suggested* (if the person has made a suggestion).

The man said (that) he didn't have anything to write about in his blog.

Note: When reporting statements, *that* is common, but optional.

Changes in Pronouns

In order to make it clear that the reported statement was made by someone else, we may need to change some of the pronouns. In the example above, it would not be logical to use the pronouns *I* or *my* in the reported speech because they refer to the original speaker (the man).

Changes in Time

Generally, we take the tense of the verb used in the original statement and use a verb one step further in the past in the reported statement.

He said, "I don't have anything to write about in my blog." (direct quote)

He said he didn't have anything to write about in his blog. (reported speech)

Use the meaning of the original statement to guide your decision about changing pronouns and tenses.

Exercise C

In a recent study, researchers interviewed college students to find out their entertainment habits. Below is what some students said. You want to report what these students said in an article you are writing for the school newspaper. Write each quote in reported speech:

A (female): "I had a cellphone for seven years in my teens before I gave it up."

B (male): "The only celebrity I follow on Twitter is the Canadian singer Feist. I just adore her."

C (male): "My twelve-year-old sister texts at night in bed."

D (female): "I don't think people are too obsessed with celebrities."

E (female): "My friends are too obsessed with celebrities."

F (male): "The most important thing for me is to hang out with my friends. I don't really care what we do as long as we're together."

G (male): "I'm a big music fan. Last week I downloaded fifty new songs from iTunes."

Reporting Questions

Reported questions are introduced by the reporting verb *ask*.

Examples: He *asked* if I tweeted.

He *asked* when the celebrity interview was.

A reported question is a statement, not a question. Therefore, the order of the words in a reported question is the same as in a statement.

Yes/No questions

We use *if*, not *that*, to introduce reported yes/no questions. *That* is optional when reporting statements. *If* is not optional when reporting questions.

Example: Quoted: Do you tweet?
Reported: He asked if I tweeted.

Information questions

The question word (*who what, where, when, how, why*) that introduces an information question, also introduces the reported information question.

Example: Quoted: *When* is the celebrity interview?
Reported: She asked *when* the celebrity interview was.

Exercise D

Audiences love to hear from their favourite celebrities on talk shows. Here are some questions the talk show host asked a famous musician. Report the questions.

1. How do you describe your musical style?
    The host . . .
2. How long have you been playing music?
    The host . . .
3. Do you play any other instruments?
    The host . . .

4. Do you like touring?
    The host . . .
5. Why do you think you are so successful?
    The host . . .

Exercise E

Read the conversation and answer the questions.

John: Did you see the latest episode of *Dig In*?
Mary: Yeah, I saw it.
Natasha: I don't know what you're talking about. I've never even heard of that show.
Luke: I don't believe it! You've never seen an episode of *Dig In*?
Melissa: You know I haven't seen it yet either, but I've heard it's great. I'm going to start watching it next week.
Natasha: What night is it on?

1. What did John ask?
2. What did Mary say about last night's episode?
3. What did Natasha say about the show?
4. What did Melissa say?
5. What did Natasha ask?

Reporting sentences with modals

The rules for changing tenses also apply to modals used in the present tense.

Direct quote: "I can meet you online in an hour to play the game."
Reported speech: Her friend said he could meet her online in an hour to play the game.

Note: Do not change past modals to past perfect modals.

Exercise F

Last week Mindy met a famous actor who had been in town for a film festival. Mindy's friend Ivan reported the story to Sandi over the phone. Read what Ivan told Sandi. Pay attention to the ten examples of reported speech. Then, write the original dialogue as it might have been. You will have to write some additional sentences for the dialogue, but make sure you include the direct speech sentences from the telephone conversation.

Hey Sandi. You'll never believe what happened to Mindy last week. You know how we have this fantastic film festival in Toronto? Well last week Mindy walked into a coffee shop downtown and who do you think was sitting there? Alfonso Bandoro, that crazy new actor from Brazil. Of course, she went right over to his table and (1) she asked if he was Alfonso Bandoro. It was really him. Then (2) she asked if he was here for the premiere of his new film and (3) he said, yes, he was. She (4) asked if it was his first time in Toronto, and (5) he said it was. (6) He said he usually goes to Montreal when he visits Canada. You won't believe this but (7) she asked him if she could take a picture of the two of them with her cellphone and he agreed. So now she has a photo of the two of them on her Facebook page, so check it out. That's not all. After she took the picture, (8) she told him that she had a friend, Sandi (that's you), who followed him on Twitter who had told her that he had a new girlfriend. (9) She asked him if that was true. Guess what? (10) He said no, he didn't have a new girlfriend, he had a new wife. He's married! Can you believe it? Hot off the press! Ok, that's my great new story. How are things with you?

Grammar in Use

Work with a partner to perform a role play. Imagine you meet your favourite star in a restaurant. Write a short dialogue of about eight to ten lines. Check that the sentences are grammatically correct. Then, form a group of six. Perform your dialogues for each other. After each role play you observe, report one thing each person said, both orally and in writing.

Vocabulary

What Entertains Us?

What words do you already know? Write three or four words for each picture that people use to talk about these things. Share your words with a partner and add any new words to your group of words.

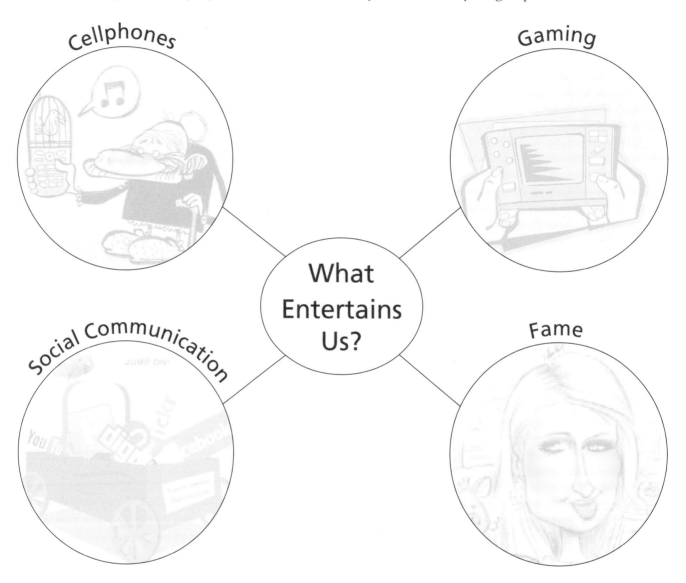

Exercise A

Some vowels are missing from each word. Add vowels to make full words. Then, add the words to the pictures above.

1. bl_gg_ng
2. c_l_br_ty
3. c_mmun_ty
4. c_nn_ct_d
5. d_v_c_s
6. fe_t_r_s
7. g_m_ng
8. g_nr_
9. hyp_
10. l_rk_ng
11. m_d_a
12. n_tw_rk_ng
13. t_xt_ng
14. tr_nds
15. tw__t

Exercise B

Read the sentences and complete the crossword puzzle with the words from the list in Exercise A.

Across

3. One reason games remain so popular is that companies are always adding new _____ to improve the game. For example, in role playing games characters can do more things, players can get more gaming points,– the possibilities are endless.

4. _____ is a way to have your opinion and stories heard by many people over the Internet. We no longer have to rely on big media companies to decide what the public will hear and not hear.

6. In the last half of the decade there was a lot of _____ about Twitter, a service that allows you to post messages of up to 140 characters. Everyone was talking about it in the media.

8. Television, radio, and newspapers are traditional media. The Internet and mobile phones are called *new* _____.

10. Technology is changing so quickly that no one can really predict what the future entertainment _____ will be.

12. Social-networking sites like Facebook or MySpace create a _____. People like the feeling of belonging to a group.

14. Reality TV is a popular program _____ around the world.

15. _____ is the most common activity on cell-phones.

Down

1. New media is an important form of entertainment because of its social _____ ability. It brings people together.

2. More and more people want to know every detail of the professional and personal lives of rich and famous people. Some people think this interest is

healthy, but others think it is not. This extreme interest even has a special name. It's called _____ worship.

5. Console and online _____ is still a popular form of entertainment. Will the popularity of *World of Warcraft* ever die?

7. With social media people can stay up to date with what's happening with their friends and famous people. They can communicate with each other any time and instantly. It makes people feel _____.

9. Mattel introduced the first hand-held electronic game in 1977, but hand-held gaming _____ became really popular when Nintendo came out with Game Boy in 1989.

11. Members of online communities generally don't like it when strangers follow what is going on in their community. _____ in online communities is a little like a stranger looking into the window of your home to see what your family is doing.

13. Many movie and TV stars _____ on Twitter to communicate with their fans.

Exercise C

Complete the chart. Include the plural ending for noun forms.

Activity	Noun		Verb
	Singular	Plural	
blogging			
connecting			
featuring			
gaming			
lurking	~~~	~~~	
networking			
texting			
tweeting			
~~	celebrity		~~~
~~	community		~~~
~~	device		~~~
~~	genre		~~~
~~		~~~	hype
~~	trend		~~~

Vocabulary in Use

Work in teams. Use the Nielsen Research Report on pages 40–44. In ten minutes, write as many true statements as you can about how teens use media, using the vocabulary words above. Do not copy sentences from the text. Your team will get one point for every sentence it has that no other team has.

Listening

Before You Listen

Discuss the questions in small groups.

1. How do you know what your friends are doing or thinking?
2. Who are your favourite celebrities? How do you know what your favourite stars are doing or thinking?
3. Do you think some celebrities use social media to sell themselves? Which celebrities do you think use media this way?

Listening

You will hear a CBC (Canadian Broadcasting Corporation) radio interview with Canadian social critic and writer Hal Niedzviecki. Shelagh Rogers is the host of the program.

> "Have you noticed lately that the tabloids have moved movie stars off the front cover and replaced them with people from reality TV? Well, this need to consume the details of a stranger's life is at the centre of Hal Niedzviecki's book *The Peep Diaries: How We're Learning to Love Watching Ourselves and Our Neighbours.* Hal joins me now from Toronto."

Excerpt 1—From Pop to Peep

Listening for Specific Information

Host Shelagh Rogers asks Hal what the difference is between pop culture and peep culture. Listen to understand the difference between the two.

Check whether each statement describes pop culture or peep culture.

Pop	Peep	
☐	☐	1. We are entertained by watching other people perform.
☐	☐	2. We are spending more and more of our leisure time watching other people go about their everyday lives.
☐	☐	3. We're watching celebrities go shopping or sleep or pick their nose, or do whatever it is they're going to do that day.
☐	☐	4. We used to watch a celebrity act or do their song and dance.
☐	☐	5. We want to watch celebrities get divorced, get arrested, get drunk, go shopping, and buy a coffee.
☐	☐	6. We don't need to be a celebrity with special talents to get attention.
☐	☐	7. We can project our own everyday problems and we can get attention that way.

Excerpt 2—Twitter

1. Hal interviewed the founders of Twitter several years ago. At that time, did Hal believe that Twitter would be successful?

   ☐ Yes ☐ No ☐ He wasn't sure

2. What did critics say about Twitter when the service first came to the market? Check all the correct statements.

   ☐ a) Twitter will never have more than about five thousand users.

   ☐ b) Twitter is a fad.

   ☐ c) Twitter is stupid.

   ☐ d) People won't be interested in what someone has for breakfast.

   ☐ e) No one can predict if Twitter will be successful.

   ☐ f) Not enough people will use it to make it economically successful.

3. What reason did the founders of Twitter give for predicting its success?

   ☐ a) Twitter will allow people to connect to as many friends as possible.

   ☐ b) Twitter allows users to connect, but not have any obligation to each other.

   ☐ c) People want to connect with their favourite celebrities.

Excerpt 3—The Story

Listening to Retell

1. Write key words to help you remember the story. In pairs, retell the story.

For Discussion

1. Hal says that peep culture is the evolution of pop culture. How do you think peep culture evolved from pop culture?

2. Do you agree with the reason the founders of Twitter gave for its predicted success? Explain your opinion.

3. What lesson does the story teach?

Thinking outside the Box

1. Hal agrees with the founders of Twitter about the reason for its popularity. What if they are wrong, however? What other reasons could explain its popularity?

2. Hal believes that we live in a peep culture. He explains what he means by peep culture and gives reasons for the attraction of peep culture. Think about your own preferences for entertainment. In what ways do your personal experiences support (agree with) or refute (disagree with) Hal's ideas?

Unit Reflection

Consider what you have learned about the media habits and preferences of youth around the world, the attraction of social media, celebrity worship, and peep culture. In small groups, brainstorm a new entertainment concept that will attract young consumers.

Unit 5
Buyer Beware!

DISCUSSION

1. Describe the best deal you got this year.
2. Describe the worst deal you got this year.
3. As a class, determine the best and worst deals of the group.

Vocabulary

Exercise A

The words or expressions in the green box deal with shopping. Use your dictionary to find the meanings of words you don't know. Then copy the categories below and write the words or expressions on the appropriate shopping bag.

discount, deal, warranty, knock off, counterfeit, sales pitch, consumer, receipt, store credit, scam, recall, promotions, wholesale/retail, telemarketer, return policy, contract, refund

Products/Purchases

Faulty/Illegal Products

Marketing/Advertising

Exercise B

Choose the statement that best explains the meaning of each sentence.

1. Most fitness centres require you to sign a contract for a year-long gym membership.
   a) The legal agreement is a commitment to pay membership fees for one year.
   b) The agreement can be changed at any time during the year.
   c) The centre signs an agreement for a year for a centre membership.

2. Cheap knock offs are counterfeits of an original product.
   a) The products are the same quality and price.
   b) The copies look the same as the original, but they are illegal products.
   c) The products are manufactured by the original company, but are for a cheaper market.

3. Store owners buy products in bulk at a wholesale store and resell the items individually in their retail stores.
   a) Only large-sized products are sold to store owners in wholesale stores.
   b) Consumers can purchase individual items at either a wholesale or a retail store.
   c) Store owners purchase items at cheaper prices in large quantities and then sell them for more money in their stores.

4. Telemarketers often call you in the evening when you are likely to be home.
   a) They are trying to sell you a product.
   b) They are trying to gather information about your shopping habits.
   c) They are trying to see if you are at home in the evenings.

5. Many electronics stores try to sell you extended warranties on items you purchase.
   a) When you purchase electronics, you must also purchase a warranty to protect you from faulty products and guarantee free repairs for a specific period of time.
   b) Retailers want you to purchase an extra period of warranty that protects you from faulty products, but it is optional.
   c) There is no automatic manufacturer warranty on electronics so if you want a warranty, you have to purchase it.

6. You get a better deal if you purchase the fridge and stove together. You even get free delivery.
   a) Companies can buy special products and sell them to you.
   b) Companies offer a special price if you buy a certain product or group of products.
   c) Companies offer a single product for the same price as a group of products.

7. The return policy states that this store only gives store credits, not refunds, when you return an item.
   a) If you return an item, you get a credit from the store for the value to spend on a different item.
   b) If you return an item, the store puts the amount back on your credit card.
   c) If you return an item, the store gives you cash for your return.

8. My friend was the victim of a scam that tricked her into sending money in order to receive a big prize. She never received the prize.
   a) An illegal con artist talked her into paying money to get a big prize, but she didn't send the money.
   b) A con artist talked her into sending money to win a big prize, but it was a fake contest.
   c) A con artist talked her into paying money and then sent her only a small prize instead of a big prize.

9. The company has issued a recall for its product because many people were hurt by it.
   a) The company is renaming the product.
   b) The company is asking consumers to return the product to the store where they purchased it because the product is dangerous.
   c) The company is apologizing to the people for their injuries.

10. In order to get a discount on the soap, you have to show your receipt for the purchase of three tubes of toothpaste.
    a) If you buy the soap, you get a receipt for toothpaste.
    b) If you provide a receipt for the toothpaste, you can get a cheaper price on the soap.
    c) If you get the soap cheaper, you can purchase toothpaste.

Vocabulary in Use

In pairs, write and role play the following guided dialogues. Use words from the vocabulary exercises.

Shopping Retail	
The Sales Clerk	**The Customer**
Ask the customer questions about why he or she has come to your store and respond to his or her questions. You can add other information.	*Answer the sales clerk's questions by using the following prompts.*
offer help	purchase a cellphone
describe choices	request recommendation
give recommendation	return policy?
2 weeks with receipt	manufacturer's warranty?
3 months – offer extended warranty	repairs? where?
return to store – length of time for repair	purchase
price	pay
thanks (end transaction)	take leave

Telemarketing	
Consumer	**Telemarketer**
Answer the telemarketer's questions by using the following notes.	*Try to sell a newspaper subscription.*
answer phone confirm your identity respond positively not interested cost? cancel? agree number end call	request Mr./Mrs. _____ greeting—read paper? have great introductory offer almost free, pay weekends only $2/week—6 months cancel anytime credit-card number thanks (end call)

Reading

Before You Read

Work in pairs to discuss the following questions:

1. Do you consider yourself to be always / usually / sometimes / rarely / never careful with your money? What or who has influenced how you spend money?

2. What are the main influences that convince you to buy an item that you were not planning to purchase?

Jigsaw Reading

Divide into two teams. Each team will read either "Ways Stores Get You to Spend More Than You Think" or "Phone Scams to Get Your Money" and answer the questions that follow. Then form pairs with one person from the other team and tell your partner about the reading. Use the information in the class discussion that follows.

Ways Stores Get You to Spend More Than You Think

Retailers try to get you into their stores by advertising low prices. But once inside, there are many strategies that store owners use to separate you from your money. Who isn't tempted to purchase more than they intended when they see great sales, double discounts and buy-one-get-one-free advertisements? When it comes to shopping, it is a case of "buyer beware."

Double Discounts

Retailers know that most people aren't good at math, and they take advantage of this. Many shopkeepers use double discounts to earn more money while making customers think they are getting a better deal than they actually are. For example, if you are given a choice of buying a one-hundred-dollar item at 45 percent off, or buying the same item at 20 percent off with an additional 30 percent taken off at the cash register, which would you choose? Most people simply add the 20 and 30 percent and assume that they are getting 50 percent off the item. When you do the math, however, it doesn't work out that way. Taking 45 percent off of one hundred dollars means the item sells for fifty dollars. On the other hand, taking 20 percent off one hundred leaves you with eighty dollars. Then 30 percent off that eighty dollars is an additional twenty-four-dollar discount. The total discount is twenty dollars plus twenty four dollars for a total discount of forty-four dollars. The item would sell for fifty-six, or a dollar more than the 45 percent discount. Most people, however, mistakenly think the double discount is a better deal.

"Sale" Doesn't Mean a Discount Price

Retailers use your beliefs about sales to sell items. Consumers are trained to think that "sale" means a lower price and sale items are usually advertised in big, bright lettering at the end of store aisles. The problem is that what the stores call a "sale" may not give you a very good price. You may see an item "on sale" and buy the product assuming it's a good price, but it may not really be a special price.

Buy One, Get One Free

This is another promotion that can mislead you into thinking you're getting a good deal. It's often difficult to tell whether you would pay half as much for purchasing a single unit or whether the price of a single unit has been increased to include the cost of the extra item being "given away." Many times the buy-one-get-one-free offers are not better than the regular price of purchasing two items.

Reading for the Main Idea

1. Select the statement that best states the main idea.
   a) Retailers try to trick consumers with false sales advertising.
   b) Consumers do not always interpret sales advertising correctly.
   c) Consumers believe that sale items are priced lower than the item's regular price.
   d) Retailers want consumers to purchase most items at a sale price.
2. Note the main points that you will use to summarize the reading for your partner. Use your own words.

For Discussion

Work in small groups to answer the following questions:

1. Why is it understandable that many consumers think a double discount is a better deal?
2. Is it illegal to raise the price of a single item when offering a buy-one-get-one-free deal? Is it ethical?
3. Why do stores put sale items at the end of aisles? Are sale items always cheaper? How are these sales advertised to shoppers?

Phone Scams to Get Your Money

1 The phone rings. At the other end of the line is a skilled con artist—an individual that wants to trick you out of your money. These dishonest people have several convincing stories to tell when you answer the 5 phone. One of the most popular and successful is the "Sweepstakes Pitch" scam. Another scam that targets the elderly is the "Grandchild in Trouble" story. These fraudsters are very convincing at getting you to "buy" their stories. When someone calls you on the 10 phone and tells you to pay money, it is a case of "buyer beware."

The Sweepstakes Pitch

One of the most common scams is the "Sweepstakes Pitch." When you answer the phone, you are told that you have won a prize in a sweepstakes. The caller tells 15 you that he is a lawyer or some other official. He is really excited because you are one of the grand-prize winners. And the prize is big—usually a new car or cash. You get excited, too—who doesn't like winning?

As your excitement increases, the caller tells you that 20 before you can receive your prize, you have to pay the taxes. You may need to pay several hundred dollars or even a thousand or more, but your prize is worth twenty times that. You really want the prize. Before you know it, you have either given your credit-card 25 information to the caller or mailed the money to the sweepstakes company. You wait, but the prize never arrives.

Emergency or "Grandparent" Scam

Another common scam takes advantage of the elderly. They receive a phone call from someone who 30 greets them as Grandma or Grandpa when they answer the phone. The caller then asks if the grandparent knows who is calling. Usually the grandparent says the name of a grandchild, which the caller confirms. The grandchild is very upset and is in seri- 35 ous trouble. He says that he has been in a serious car accident or has had some kind of serious problem while travelling abroad and needs cash urgently. He begs his grandparent to send him money immediately through a money transfer company. He spe- 40 cifically asks the grandparent not to tell his parents because he doesn't want them to find out he is in trouble. Wanting to help the grandchild, the grandparent hurries to the bank and then sends the money. It is only after not hearing from the grandchild after 45 a few days that the grandparent contacts family members. That is when the grandparents discover that their grandchild never called them. It was all a scam to get money from them.

Reading for the Main Idea

1. Select the statement that best states the main idea of the reading.
   a) All calls that inform you that you have won a prize are scams.
   b) The elderly are easier to trick than other age groups.
   c) Callers use your emotions to try and get you to spend money.
   d) There are several telephone scams that get you to give your credit card or send money to a company.
2. Note the main points that you will use to summarize the reading for your partner. Use your own words.

For Discussion

Work in small groups to answer the following questions:

1. What makes the "Sweepstakes Pitch" phone call believable?
2. Is it illegal to keep the money when people have voluntarily sent the money or given their credit-card number? Is it ethical?
3. What do all these telephone con artists do to convince people to give them money? What makes them successful?

Class Discussion (Teams A and B)

How do telemarketers and retailers use their knowledge of consumer beliefs and behaviours to sell you products?

Thinking outside the Box

Create a "Buyer Beware" TV advertisement that informs newcomers about misleading sales and other scams.

SNAPSHOPT OF CANADA 📷

The Canadian Anti-Fraud Centre (CAFC) in North Bay, Ontario—more commonly known as Phone Busters—is the central agency in Canada that collects information and criminal intelligence on mass-marketing fraud, identity theft complaints, and Internet fraud.

Pronunciation Power

Joining words together is known as linking. Linking helps to make English speech sound smooth.

- When one word ends with a consonant sound that is the same as the consonant sound that begins the next word, the two consonant sounds are combined to sound like one long consonant. The two words sound like one.

  Example: some money /m/ + /ˈm/ /səm/ + /ˈmʌni/

- When one word ends with a consonant sound and the next word begins with a vowel sound, the final consonant sound is linked to the vowel.

  Example: banking official /ŋ/ + /ə/ /ˈbaŋkiŋ/ + /əˈfiʃl/

- When a word that ends with a tense vowel sound such as /i/ (me), /ɪ/ (stay), /oː/(go), or /uː/ (blue) is followed by a word that begins with a vowel sound, the words are linked by a /j/ (yes) or /w/ (white).

  Examples: money order /ˈmʌni/ + /ˈoːdər/

  she isn't /ʃi/ + /ˈɪznt/

Exercise A

a) Listen to the sentences warning you about scams. Mark the linking that you hear.
b) State the linking rule.
c) Take turns reading the sentences to a partner using linking.

1. If it sounds too good to be true, it is.
2. Legitimate sweepstakes don't require a fee. You should never have to pay before playing.
3. Beware if someone asks for personal financial information.
4. If someone asks for cash or a money order, it is probably a scam.
5. If the caller is more excited than you are, you should be suspicious.
6. Don't believe it when a person claims to be a government official, tax officer, banking official, lawyer, or some other person in authority.
7. Don't trust a caller that wants to be your friend.
8. When someone tells you the deal is a time-limited offer and you must act now—act! Hang up!

Exercise B

1. Write five warning sentences that you would tell others so they don't get tricked.

2. Draw a line to connect the sounds that are linked between the words.

3. Practise saying the sentences to a partner.

Speaking

In small groups, discuss the advantages and disadvantages of purchasing knock offs.

Grammar Focus

Exercise A

1I really enjoy **watching** _sports_ on a big screen television. Last week I decided to upgrade our old TV to a large flat screen. 2**Purchasing** a TV is not easy. 3I didn't plan on **taking** _so long_ at the store to make a decision. There are so many brands of televisions to choose from and each has different features. 4**Researching** _the products_ before you go is a good idea. 5I told the sales person that I was interested in **hearing** _his opinion_ about a particular model. 6He was very **convincing.** I decided to buy it. I asked about the warranty. He said that it came with a manufacturer's warranty that covered some potential problems for one year. 7**Buying** _an extended warranty_ was highly recommended. 8I hadn't planned on **spending** _extra money_ for a warranty. Many people think that warranties are just a way for retailers to get more money from you. 9They think that buying a warranty is **throwing away** _your money_. 10I thought about not **getting** _the extra warranty_ but the sales clerk convinced me that it was wise because repairs could be very expensive. I still don't know if I did the right thing. When it comes to warranties, it is "buyer beware." Only time will tell if the warranty was worth the extra two hundred dollars.

- Look at the words in bold. What do they all have in common in terms of meaning?
- Look at the underlined phrases. What relationship do the italicized words have to the bolded word in each phrase?

1. What parts of speech are the bolded words?
2. Identify the grammatical function in the sentence for each bolded word.
3. Write the base word used to form each bolded word. What do you notice about changes in spelling?

Gerunds and Gerund Phrases

A gerund indicates an action or a state of being. A gerund is a verbal: it is a verb form, but it does not act like a verb in a sentence—it functions as a noun. It can have the same position in the sentence as other nouns. The gerund can be a subject, a direct object, or an object of a preposition. A gerund phrase contains the object of the gerund or any words used to modify it.

1. The gerund can be the subject of the sentence. Note: The gerund in the subject position is always singular. The gerund can be replaced by the pronoun _it_.

    Subject
    Purchasing a computer is expensive.

2. The gerund can be the subject complement.

    Subject complement
    _His sales pitch is _convincing_.

3. The gerund can be the object of certain verbs. There is no pattern or rule—you need to memorize these verbs. See Appendix page 152 for a list.

   I dislike <u>purchasing extended warranties</u>.
   I recommend <u>researching the product first</u>.

4. The gerund (G) always follows a preposition (P) if you want to indicate an action or state of being. It is the object of the preposition.

P G
Do you have any opinions about <u>purchasing extended warranties</u>?

V + P G
I plan on <u>purchasing a television</u>.

adj. + P G
I'm tired of <u>spending money</u> on warranties I never use.

Exercise B

1. Rewrite the following sentences using a gerund or gerund phrase.

   Example: It usually costs a lot to buy an extended warranty.

   <u>Buying</u> <u>an extended warranty</u> *usually costs a lot.*

   a) It must be difficult to sell expensive electronic items.

   b) It might be a good idea to purchase a warranty.

   c) It is really important to read the fine print before you purchase something.

   d) It would be unfortunate to not have a warranty if the computer broke down.

   e) It is challenging to make the right decision.

   f) It should be enjoyable to watch your new TV for the first time.

Exercise C

Write a summary sentence for each pair of statements. Use the correct form of a verb from the following list and the gerund form of the verb in parentheses.

admit *(agree that something about your behaviour is true)*
delay *(put off until later)*
consider *(think about something carefully)*
enjoy *(take pleasure in)*
mention *(speak about quickly)*
mind *(object to someone/something)*
postpone *(put off until later)*
report *(tell about)*
regret *(feel sorry for something you have done)*
risk *(take the chance that something harmful will happen)*

1. She claims he told her that the product was on sale. He said that was true.

   He *<u>admitted telling</u>* her that the product was on sale.
   (tell)

2. If you buy this television, you'll be getting a really good deal. Please think about it.

   Please _____ this television
   (purchase)
   because it's a good deal.

3. She likes to buy things on sale. It makes her feel good.

   She _____ for sales.
   (shop)

4. I bought the extended warranty. I wish I hadn't done that.

   I _____ the extended warranty.
   (buy)

5. I was going to buy a computer. I think I'll wait a month.

   I think I'll _____ the computer
   (purchase)
   until next month.

6. If you don't have a warranty, you are taking a chance. The repairs can be expensive.

   Without a warranty, you _____
   (pay)
   for an expensive repair.

7. He briefly talked about that TV model. He said it had a lot of problems.

   He _____ a lot of problems with
   (have)
   that TV model.

8. I would like that in writing. That isn't a problem, is it?

   Do you _____ that in writing?
   (put)

Exercise D

In the following sentences, highlight the gerund and underline the gerund phrases. Identify the function of each gerund phrase.

a) object of a verb
b) object of a phrasal verb (verb + participle or verb + preposition)
c) object of a preposition or prepositional phrase
d) subject of the sentence
e) subject complement

1. _d_ <u>Watching my new TV</u> is a waste of time.
2. ___ He has strong opinions about advertising to children.
3. ___ Let's talk about doing a cost comparison.
4. ___ Don't delay making a decision.
5. ___ He ended up returning the television.
6. ___ She wrote a magazine article about buying cellphones.
7. ___ She put off making a decision.
8. ___ It would depend on getting a good price.
9. ___ Buying an extended warranty is not worth it.
10. ___ It is rewarding to finish the job.

Grammar in Use

Create a "Buyer Beware" brochure for newcomers to Canada. Include as many meaningful sentences as possible using a word or phrase from each column.

Example: Instead of relying on a friend's opinion, research the product yourself.

instead of	research the product
insist on	read the warranty
think about	waste my money
be worried about	purchase a computer
it's no use	buy a television
depend on	get an extended warranty
in addition to	pay more for added coverage
before	visit the store
end up	ask a friend
suggest	worry about
	pay too much

Listening

Before You Listen

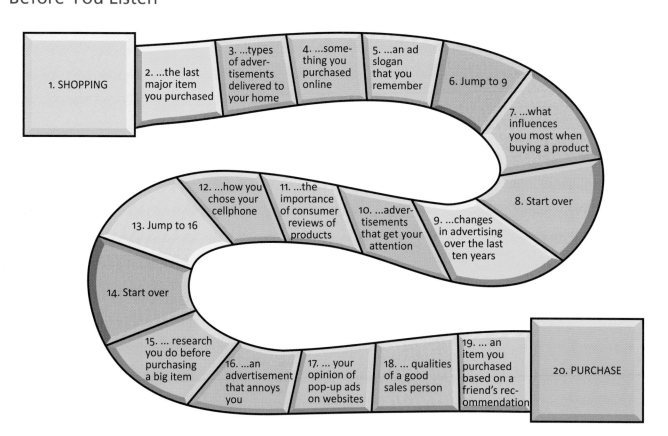

1. SHOPPING
2. ...the last major item you purchased
3. ...types of advertisements delivered to your home
4. ...something you purchased online
5. ...an ad slogan that you remember
6. Jump to 9
7. ...what influences you most when buying a product
8. Start over
9. ...changes in advertising over the last ten years
10. ...advertisements that get your attention
11. ...the importance of consumer reviews of products
12. ...how you chose your cellphone
13. Jump to 16
14. Start over
15. ... research you do before purchasing a big item
16. ...an advertisement that annoys you
17. ... your opinion of pop-up ads on websites
18. ... qualities of a good sales person
19. ... an item you purchased based on a friend's recommendation
20. PURCHASE

Play the game in small groups. You need a place marker for each person and one die for the group.

1. Roll the die and move your marker ahead the number of spaces shown on the die.
2. Talk about the subject on the spaces that you landed on for thirty seconds. Example, if you land on space 4, talk about "something you purchased online" for thirty seconds.
3. Take turns rolling the die and moving around the board.
4. If you can't talk about the subject for thirty seconds, return to your previous space.
5. If you land on a **Jump** space, discuss the topic on the new space. If you land on **Start over**, return to the **SHOPPING** square—you do not have to talk.
6. When a player reaches **PURCHASE**, the game is finished.

Listening for the Main Idea

1. Listen to a research focus group meeting with young people who belong to the "Net Generation." This is the generation of people who are currently between the ages of eleven and thirty-one. They are discussing what influences their purchases. The first excerpt is a general introduction of the participants. What is the topic of discussion in excerpts 2, 3, and 4?
2. Decide which of the following sentences best summarizes the group's discussion.
   a) The Net Generation makes most of its major purchases online.
   b) Net Generation consumers are quite savvy. They research a product extensively before they make a purchase and they don't trust traditional forms of marketing.
   c) Net Generation consumers do a lot of research and prefer infomercials that tell them about all the features of a product.
   d) Advertising through social networking sites like Facebook and Twitter is as effective as infomercials and glossy brochures.

Listening for Specific Information

Take notes for Lois. Use the following outline as a guide.

Excerpt 1

	Age	Occupation	Purchase
Anastasia			
Mei Tin			
Martin			
Salim			

Excerpt 2

Influences

_____
_____
_____
_____
_____
_____

Excerpt 3

	Purchase Online? Y/N	Why?
Anastasia		
Mei Tin		
Martin		
Salim		

Excerpt 4

Two ways marketers try to get their product known to the Net Generation
1.
2.

Summarizing

Lois wrote the following executive summary for the research company. Fill in the missing details using your notes.

Executive Summary

The traditional way of marketing through multi-media advertising, direct-mail campaigns, infomercials, and other one-way communication techniques is not effective with the Net Generation. Net Generation consumers are very savvy. They $_1$ _____ before making a purchase. Generally, they do not $_2$ _____, mainly because they do not have credit cards and they prefer to $_3$ _____ at the store. This generation's consumers rely on the advice of their $_4$ _____ and social media. They check out the buzz on a product and are very knowledgeable about $_5$ _____ of the product they are purchasing. They know where they can get the best price. This generation is aware that consumers cannot trust everything they read. Some are aware of new ways marketers try to sell their products to them such as using $_6$ _____ and $_7$ _____. To successfully market to this generation, it is important to present things honestly, include them in product decisions, and create a buzz for a product.

Thinking outside the Box

Describe the most effective advertising campaign that targets the Net Generation.

If you are not satisfied with a product, you should first try to solve the problem at the store where you purchased it. If you are not satisfied with the store's response, you can write a letter of complaint to the company that made the product.

A complaint letter includes the following information:

- your full address, telephone number, and the date of writing the letter;
- a greeting;
- the purpose of your letter;
- the name, model, and serial number of the product;
- the place and date you purchased the product, and the price you paid;
- a description of the problem with the product: What is the problem? When did the problem start?;
- the rules of the warranty;
- a description of the actions you have taken to try to fix the problem and the result;
- a statement that describes what action you want the company to take (e.g., give you a refund or repair the product) and the date by which you want the problem resolved; and
- a closing phrase with your name and signature.

Note: Include a copy of your receipt and the warranty certificate.

Your situation:

Buy Lot		
23 November 2012		
9740 Irvine Boulevard		
	Model	**Price**
01.	Brand-Co LCD Television Serial #919665038204	$500
Warranty: One Year		

You purchased a television with a one-year warranty. One week after the warranty expired, the TV stopped working. The clerk at the store where you bought it told you that you needed to pay the full cost of the repairs because the warranty was finished. Rewrite the following letter by replacing the underlined information with specific information required to make the letter effective.

12/02/2013

Jason Altman
1666 Union Square
Bethany, Manitoba R0J 0E0

Buy Lot
9740 Irvine Boulevard
Bethany, Manitoba R0J 0D0

To whom it may concern:

Re: Product Complaint

Earlier, I bought a television model at a store.

Unfortunately, your product has not performed well. I am disappointed because the TV stopped after I bought it. I paid a lot of money for the TV.

In an attempt to resolve this problem, I returned the TV. The clerk at the store looked at the warranty and said no.

To resolve this problem, I would appreciate it if you would pay because you should. I am enclosing copies.

I look forward to your reply and a resolution to my problem sometime. Please contact me at the above address or telephone number.

Sincerely,

Jason Altman

Jason Altman

Unit Reflection

Summarize the top three consumer tips that you would pass on to friends so they don't waste their money.

Unit 6
Catch Me If You Can

DISCUSSION

1. What is a criminal? What are the major influences that lead someone into a life of crime?

2. What skills or knowledge do you need to solve crimes?

3. Crime scene investigation television programs are very popular. What makes them so interesting to watch? Do the programs show what really happens in crime scene investigations?

Would You Make a Good CSI?

Try the following quiz to find out if you have the knowledge it takes to be a good crime-scene investigator (CSI). Then, check your answers against those below and see how you scored.

1. Which three patterns are used to classify all fingerprints?

   loop   circle   arch   whorl   spiral

   a) loop, circle, arch
   b) arch, loop, whorl
   c) whorl, loop, spiral

2. What type of animal hair is often used to make fingerprint brushes?
   a) camel
   b) squirrel
   c) boar (male pig)

3. What causes fingerprints to occur when we touch something?
   a) salt that is present in our sweat
   b) natural oils in the skin
   c) dirt on our fingertips

4. When do human beings develop unique fingerprints?
   a) six months before birth
   b) at birth
   c) at six months of age

5. What is the study of guns and bullets called?
   a) gunshot analysis
   b) ballistics
   c) weapons study

6. A secondary crime scene is
   a) the location where two different crimes happened.
   b) the location where a second crime happened committed by the same person.
   c) an alternate location where additional evidence can be found.

7. According to crime-scene rules, which of the following should happen first?
   a) Examine the crime scene for evidence, including point of entry and exit and the general layout of the crime scene.
   b) Interview the victim or first officer on the scene to find out what happened and how the crime was committed.
   c) Take photos of the crime scene including overall shots and items of evidence.

8. Crime scene technicians wear white body suits that cover their entire body and hair because
   a) white helps them easily see and pieces of evidence get stuck on their clothing.
   b) the white body suit is comfortable and makes it easy to crawl on the floor.
   c) the white body suit is sterile and will not allow fibres or hair from the technician to become part of the crime scene.

9. Experts can use pictures and measurements of blood spatters to tell
   a) the distance from which the victim was shot.
   b) the victim's blood type.
   c) the total amount of blood that the victim lost.

10. Every cell in our body contains
   a) the same DNA.
   b) different DNA depending on the location in the body.
   c) the same DNA as our mother.

If you scored:

10: You will be a great CSI—they can't make mistakes or they'll get fired.

7–9: With some training you could be solving crimes soon!

4–6: You are either a potential CSI or a lucky guesser—time will tell.

0–3: Well, you might not be a good CSI—maybe you can get a job playing one on TV.

Answers: 1. b, 2. a, 3. b, 4. a, 5. b, 6. c, 7. b, 8. c, 9. a, 10. a

Vocabulary

Exercise A

The words or expressions below deal with a criminal investigation. Use your dictionary to check the meanings of words you don't know. Write the words in the appropriate magnifying glasses.

abduction / kidnapping	book someone	investigate	suspect
accuse	break into	investigators	the accused
alibi	convict	murder	theft / robbery / burglary
arrest	criminal	paramedics	thief / robber
arson	detectives	photographs	vandalism
assault	eyewitness	police officer	victim
attacker	firearms	rape	
be wanted	fingerprints	shoplifting	
	forensic evidence	steal	

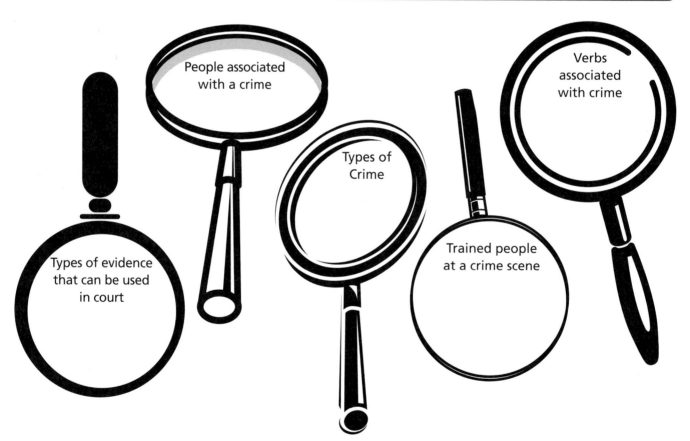

People associated with a crime

Verbs associated with crime

Types of Crime

Types of evidence that can be used in court

Trained people at a crime scene

Exercise B

Complete the following sentences using words or expressions from Exercise A.

When a crime has been committed, there is a set of rules that investigators must follow. Investigators need to gather all the possible evidence in a very careful way. This evidence can be used later at trial to help 1 _____ the person or people responsible for the crime.

   The first thing that the 2 _____ does is to interview the 3 _____ if the person is alive and can talk. The investigator wants to find out what crime happened and when. The investigator will also talk to the first 4 _____ on the scene because that cop will also be able to give valuable information about the crime.

The second step is to look for possible evidence. For example, if there was a 5 _____ , the investigator wants to determine how the 6 _____ who killed the victim entered and exited the crime scene. The investigator looks for evidence and gets an overall idea of the crime scene.

The third step is to create a digital record of the crime scene. The investigator will take 7 _____ of the crime scene and individual pictures of any visible evidence.

The fourth step is to draw a picture of the crime scene to identify the exact position of a body or other evidence. Investigators often draw a quick sketch on 8 _____ lift cards so they can record where the traces of sweat from the tips of the fingers were found.

The final step is to process the crime scene. The investigator is looking for 9 _____, which is the physical evidence that is found at a crime scene. When there is contact between two items, there will be an exchange, so the murderer will leave some evidence behind and take some evidence from the crime scene with him when he leaves. The investigator looks for strands of hair, skin cells, and fibres from clothing. The investigator collects physical evidence from the crime scene and takes it back to the crime lab for further analysis. After a careful analysis, the investigators hope they can identify a 10 _____ who they believe is responsible. The goal is to locate and convict that person for the crime.

Vocabulary in Use

Find a crime report in the newspaper. Summarize the crime story in your own words using the crime scene investigation vocabulary you have learned.

Reading

You will read about a body being discovered and about what typically happens at a crime scene.

Before You Read

Work in pairs to discuss the following:

1. Identify at least five people typically involved in a murder investigation.
2. Identify three weapons commonly used in murders.
3. List at least five types of evidence that investigators collect to help identify a killer.

Predicting

1. Scan the titles of the reading sections and write down two points you expect to read about in each section.
2. Look at the following vocabulary words. If the word is unfamiliar, look it up in a dictionary. Predict in which section you will find each word.

angles and force	live-scan machine
body	maggots
building	patterns of ridges
factory	spatters
hatch (v.)	traces
imperfections	traces of sweat
lifecycle	

The Crime Scene

A security guard shines his light in the window and sees something on the floor that looks suspicious. He calls the police and informs them that he thinks there is a body in the empty factory at the corner of Queen St. and Jones Ave. Within minutes, the police are on the scene. They quickly confirm that a crime has occurred and begin to process the crime scene. The police call in the forensic team to help them gather evidence.

Inside the building they find a body with a very visible head wound. Based on the look of the body, it has been there for at least twelve hours; however, only a careful analysis of the evidence will tell what really happened and when.

Every person, no matter how careful he is, leaves behind traces of his activities. The forensic team will be gathering important pieces of evidence including fingerprints, blood, and insect activity to help it in its investigation of the crime.

suspicious: believe something is wrong
confirm: make something definite
analysis: detailed examination
wound: body injury
trace: a tiny amount of something
forensic: science used in crime scene investigations

Comprehension Check

Is there support for the following statements in the reading? If so, underline the sentences that support the statement.

1. The security guard helped the police process the crime scene.
   Y / N
2. Police can use evidence at the scene to determine when the man was murdered.
   Y / N

Fingerprints

The first thing the team does is to fingerprint the victim. Since every individual's fingerprints are unique, this is one way to identify the victim. The forensic investigator puts the victim's fingertips on the screen of his portable live-scan machine. The images are then sent to a computer database. The forensic team also collects fingerprints from the crime scene by dusting the surfaces with a black powder. This powder sticks to the traces of sweat left behind by people when they touch a surface. The investigators lift the powdered prints with clear tape. They find some good fingerprints on the broken glass of the window. They think someone used the window to enter the factory. Later, they will run all the fingerprints through AFIS (the Automated Fingerprint Identification System) to quickly find out if there is a match to any fingerprints on file.

Over the years, experts have developed a way to distinguish fingerprints based on three patterns of ridges on the skin of the fingertip: the loop, the whorl,

Arch   Loop   Whorl

and the arch. Approximately 60 percent of people have loops, 35 percent have whorls, and 5 percent have arches. In each of these basic patterns there are small differences or imperfections. These small differences make each fingerprint unique from birth.

unique: one of a kind
identify: determine who it belongs to
dusting: lightly powder
distinguish: to show differences between things
database: collection of information saved on a computer

Comprehension Check

Is there support for the following statements in the reading? If so, underline the sentences that support the statement.

3. Special powders can be used to show the traces of sweat that remain on surfaces that we touch.
   Y / N

4. Investigators used black powder to get the victim's fingerprints.
   Y / N

Blood File

The forensic investigators also collect as much blood evidence as possible from the crime scene. There is a pool of blood around the victim's head and some dried blood spatters on the floor. The spatters show that a fight took place at least twenty-four hours previously. The officers take many close-up digital photos of the blood spatters. When drops of blood hit a surface, the shape of the mark shows the direction in which and force with which the blood was traveling. Large round drops mean that the blood fell a short distance vertically. Small blood spatters indicate that there was greater distance and force. If the blood hits an angled surface with some force, it will run and leave a tail showing which direction it came from. The forensic team uses high-tech computer programs to help it determine the angle and force of the blood as it hit the surface. Investigators use the position, shape, and size of the spatters and information from the computer analysis to find out many things. They can tell where the attacker stood, the attacker's approximate height, the number of times the victim was hit, and if the attacker was left- or right-handed.

The investigators also use a very strong light beam that produces a violet light to help them locate traces of blood that can't be seen easily. At their lab, the forensics experts will find out the blood type of the different samples to see if they all belong to the same person. They will also be able to identify individual DNA. The police use a data bank called CODIS (Combined DNA Index System) to store DNA samples. This database can be searched for matches. DNA evidence is extremely important because it can prove that an individual was

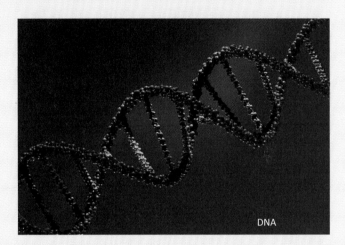

DNA

at a crime scene. Police can stop investigating suspects who do not match the DNA samples. DNA evidence is very strong because, like fingerprints, every person has unique DNA. It is very difficult to prove that DNA evidence is wrong if it is used to convict a criminal.

The investigators have to be extremely careful when gathering the evidence. They do not want to contaminate the evidence by gathering it improperly. They also have to store it carefully so it does not come into contact with any other evidence. If they do not collect, record, and store the DNA evidence according to strict guidelines, the results will not be allowed as evidence in court. The forensic team spends hours collecting as much evidence as possible before it removes the body.

---

spatters: small drops
attacker: someone who uses violence to harm
contaminate: make unusable
store: keep in safe place for future use

Comprehension Check

Is there support for the following statements in the reading? If so, underline the sentences that support the statement.

5. There was only a small amount of blood close to the victim's head.
   Y / N
6. Blood must be visible for the police to locate it.
   Y / N

Insect Evidence

The forensic team also collects some other very important evidence at the factory that will help it decide when the victim was killed. Bug experts (entomologists) can use the development of the insects that they find on the body to estimate when the victim died. Once a person dies, his cells immediately start to break down and give off a weak odour. Insects can smell this odour long before any human can.

The blowfly is a common insect all over the world. Blowflies lay their eggs in moist areas such as the mouth, nose, eyes, and wounds within minutes of someone or something dying. A female blowfly can lay hundreds of eggs. The eggs hatch into maggots. This takes between twelve and twenty-four hours depending on the temperature. The maggots feed on the body and grow to become a pupa. This can take between six and twelve days. After a period of time a new adult fly hatches from the pupa, usually in about two weeks. The time for this lifecycle depends on the temperature so investigators need to determine the temperature inside the factory.

The investigators find eggs and maggots on the body. Based on this evidence, they know that the man has been dead for at least twenty-four hours. They keep some of the maggots alive so they can take them back to the lab and watch how long it takes them to turn into pupa. This will help tell them when the murder happened. They also keep some in alcohol to be used as evidence.

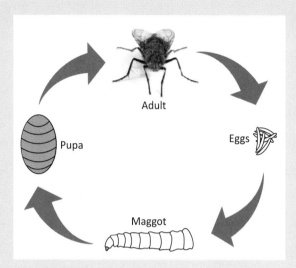

Investigators know from the condition of the body that he has been dead less than thirty-six hours. They have gathered a lot of evidence from the crime scene. They even found what they think is likely the murder weapon—an old pipe covered with blood at one end. Now it will take careful processing of all the evidence to recreate the last moments of the victim's life, but hopefully they will be able to determine who is responsible for this terrible crime.

estimate: guess using scientific evidence
detect: notice
moist: wet

Comprehension Check

Is there support for the following statements in the reading? If so, underline the sentences that support the statement.

7. Blowflies start laying their eggs on the hands and arms of a body almost immediately after death.
   Y / N
8. The police found an object at the crime scene they think was used to murder the victim.
   Y / N

Victims and Persons Accused of Homicide in Canada, by Age and Sex

	2005	2006	2007	2005	2006	2007
		Victims			Accused	
Males	483	444	432	583	484	474
0 to 11 years	22	16	14	0	1	3
12 to 17 years	19	12	23	62	73	66
18 to 24 years	108	110	119	222	149	177
25 to 29 years	86	69	60	77	78	63
30 to 39 years	84	91	78	100	85	78
40 to 49 years	80	70	62	68	57	53
50 to 59 years	45	39	39	27	22	22
60 years and over	39	36	37	27	19	12
Age not known	0	1	0	0	0	0
Females	180	162	162	63	73	53
0 to 11 years	13	16	11	0	0	0
12 to 17 years	8	16	8	10	12	8
18 to 24 years	24	24	21	19	23	12
25 to 29 years	16	16	16	6	10	8
30 to 39 years	39	32	33	19	10	17
40 to 49 years	31	23	36	5	13	4
50 to 59 years	17	20	18	3	4	3
60 years and over	32	14	19	1	1	1
Age not known	0	1	0	0	0	0

The statistics were retrieved from a 2009 Statistics Canada Report.

Reading for Specific Information

1. Read the table to answer the following questions:
   a) What gender is a murder victim most likely to be?
   b) What age range is the murder victim most likely to be from and why?
   c) What are the two most likely age groups that the accused would belong to if male? If female?
2. Which age range or ranges reflect the following?
   a) the biggest decrease in male victims between 2005 and 2007
   b) an increase in victims in 2006
   c) the same number of accused in at least two of the three years represented

Reading for Meaning

For each of the following sentences, find and highlight the sentence in the reading with a similar meaning.

1. The Crime Scene: The police can see that there has been a crime so they begin to take pictures and collect evidence.
2. Fingerprints: The police will use a computer program to see if any of the prints found at the crime scene match prints in the database.
3. Blood File: When blood hits a surface it will leave a mark that you can use to find out the direction the blood was moving.
4. Insect Evidence: Bugs are able to detect the smell before people can.

Thinking outside the Box

Trace evidence found at the crime scene is essential for convicting a person of committing a crime. What can criminals do to make sure they do not leave evidence behind?

Grammar Focus

Exercise A

In some sentences in the following paragraph, the action is emphasized and in others the doer of the action is emphasized.

1. Underline the sentences in which the doer of the action is emphasized.
2. Highlight the sentences in which the action is emphasized rather than the doer.
3. In pairs, discuss why the writer has chosen to emphasize the action rather than who did the action.

₁Police searched the area for clues. ₂The area around the factory was surrounded by yellow police tape. ₃Detectives searched the area looking for possible evidence. ₄A bloody shirt was found in a garbage can. ₅Police also found a trail of blood leading away from the factory. ₆Photographs of the blood spatters were taken. ₇The locations of the blood spatters were carefully recorded. ₈The police are currently questioning everyone who may have seen or heard something related to the crime. ₉They already have a few suspects to whom they are talking. ₁₀All conversations with the suspects are recorded. ₁₁The police can use the recordings as evidence at a trial. ₁₂Police believe they will be able to identify the murderer quickly. ₁₃They expect that an arrest will be made within the next twenty-four hours.

Passive Voice

The passive voice is used

1. to emphasize the receiver of the action rather than the doer of the action.
2. to describe a situation in which the doer of the action (the agent) is unknown or unimportant.
3. when the exact identity of the doer of the action is obvious.

Exercise B

1. Underline the subject and circle the verb(s) in each sentence. Who do you think performed the action of the verb?
2. The passive voice is used for different reasons in the following sentences. Match each sentence with the best reason from the green box.
    a) He was arrested and charged with the murder of his wife. *3*
    b) Crime scenes are always secured with yellow police tape.
    c) Fingerprints were found at the crime scene by the technicians.
    d) The window of the factory was broken.
    e) Dozens of pictures were taken of the crime scene.
    f) The robbery was recorded by the video surveillance camera.
    g) The evidence will be collected at the crime scene.
    h) The man was stabbed.
    i) You will be arrested if you are caught committing a crime.
    j) DNA evidence is used to prove a person was at the scene of the crime.

Exercise C

Identify the tense in each passive-voice sentence in Exercise B. Write the verb phrase in the chart. Write the pattern for forming the passive voice for each tense.

Present Tense	Past Tense	Future Tense
	was arrested	
		will be + V₃

Exercise D

Write the correct form of the verb in parentheses. Underline the key words that helped you determine the appropriate tense.

a) The body (discover) _____ at ten o'clock last night.

b) The crime scene (always secure) _____ by the first police officer to arrive.

c) A description of the suspect (give) _____ on the news tomorrow morning.

d) A missing child report must (broadcast) _____ when a child is missing.

e) Is it true that starting next month, your DNA (take) _____ if you are arrested?

f) This area (monitor) _____ by security cameras twenty-four hours a day.

g) The rare painting (steal) _____ last night.

h) Later today, the primary suspect (arrest) _____.

Pronunciation Power

English sentences have two types of words: (1) content words and (2) function words. Content words are the important words in the sentence because they carry meaning. Main verbs, nouns, adjectives, adverbs, question words, demonstratives, and negative auxiliaries are content words. Function words are not as important to the meaning. They help to give the sentence correct grammar. Pronouns, prepositions, conjunctions, articles, and auxiliaries are function words. The normal stress pattern emphasizes content words, giving English its rhythm. Listen to and repeat the following sentences. Notice how each sentence takes approximately the same time to say.

	POLICE		CATCH		CRIMINALS	(present tense)
the	POLICE		CATCH	the	CRIMINALS	(present tense)
	CRIMINALS	are	CAUGHT	by	POLICE	(present passive)
the	CRIMINALS	were	CAUGHT	by the	POLICE	(past passive)
the	CRIMINALS	will be	CAUGHT	by the	POLICE	(future passive)
the	CRIMINALS	can be	CAUGHT	by the	POLICE	(modal passive)
Note: the	CRIMINALS	CAN'T be	CAUGHT	by the	POLICE	(negative passive)

Exercise

Circle the content words in each sentence in Grammar Focus, Exercise D. Read the sentences, paying attention to the sentence rhythm.

Grammar in Use

Work with a partner to share a story of a solved crime that happened in your neighbourhood or that you read about in the news. Include the evidence that the police used to convict the suspect. Tell each other your stories. As you listen to your partner, write down three sentences in the passive voice about the crime or conviction. Show your sentences to your partner to check if they are correct.

Writing

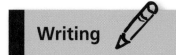

Police officers take detailed notes when they investigate a crime. These notes can be used in court to convict suspects. Imagine that you are a police officer that was at the scene of the murder described in the reading. Write detailed notes of what you saw, what you did, and how the crime scene was investigated.

Speaking

Imagine that you are a news reporter. Using the information from the police officer and potential witnesses, write a crime report for the local evening news describing what took place. In small groups, present your report and decide which version of the report told the story best.

Listening

Before You Listen

1. Write the correct number for each, based on the picture above:

   jury _____   defendant _____
   judge _____   witness _____
   juror _____   defence _____
   prosecutor _____   courtroom _____
   lawyer _____

2. In pairs, identify the following occupations. Check your answers with another group.

   a) A group of actors that play characters in a television show: c_____

   b) The person who tries to prove that the accused person is guilty of the crime: p_____

   c) The person who tries to prevent the accused person from being convicted: d_____

   d) The process of trying to determine whether an accused person is guilty: t_____

   e) The ten or more people in a courtroom responsible for unanimously deciding if someone is guilty of a crime: j_____; an individual member of this group is called a j_____.

   f) The leader of the courtroom who manages the trial: j_____

   g) An individual that is considered very knowledgeable about a subject: e_____

   h) The location where the judge has the trial: c_____

   i) An individual who has studied the laws of a country and works with those laws every day: l_____

   j) A doctor who examines dead bodies to try and determine the cause of death: p_____

k) A scientist who works with chemicals and can determine the composition of something: c_____

3. You will hear many of these words in the listening. What do you think the listening will be about?

Focused Listening

Read the following nine statements and then listen to Part 1. Circle the three statements that are not included in the listening.

1. The *CSI* franchise, *Law and Order*, *Bones*, *Criminal Minds*, and *Forensic Files* are popular crime-investigation television shows.
2. Each week more than 60 million people in countries around the world watch these popular shows.
3. The shows feature the latest technology that experts use to analyze blood spatters, fingerprints, bone fragments, tire tracks, and other trace evidence.
4. In the shows, forensic techniques such as making moulds from stab wounds to identify the type of knife used in the crime mirror real-life forensic science.
5. Forensic high-tech gadgetry is very expensive.
6. It is possible to get DNA result in just over twenty-four hours if you want to, but normally it takes several months.
7. The "*CSI* Effect" is the expectation jurors have that DNA evidence is always available to prove a case.
8. Forensic experts on television know a lot about their area of expertise and do not make mistakes.
9. In real life, the testimony of experts has led to the conviction of innocent people.

Listening for Specific Information

Listen to Part 2 to complete the following chart.

Forensic expert	Expert's occupation	Wrongfully accused/convicted person	Crime	Number of years in prison
Dr. Charles Smith		mother of slain child		
Joyce Gilchrist		Jeff Pierce		
Fred Zain		Glen Woodall		

For Discussion

1. In groups, discuss some popular crime-investigation shows that you watch. Describe similar shows from your country.
2. What makes these shows so popular?
3. What are some of the positive and negative effects that crime shows have on society?

Thinking outside the Box

A. The Canadian Charter of Rights and Freedoms describes the human rights Canadians have by law.

ALL PEOPLE IN CANADA

- MUST BE TREATED EQUALLY. A PERSON CANNOT DISCRIMINATE AGAINST ANOTHER PERSON BECAUSE OF RACE, NATIONAL OR ETHNIC ORIGIN, COLOUR, RELIGION, SEX, AGE, OR MENTAL OR PHYSICAL DISABILITY.
- MUST BE TOLD QUICKLY OF WHAT CRIMES THEY ARE ACCUSED
- MUST BE CONSIDERED INNOCENT UNTIL THEY ARE PROVEN GUILTY
- HAVE THE RIGHT TO A SPEEDY TRIAL
- HAVE THE RIGHT TO AN INTERPRETER IF THEY DO NOT SPEAK ONE OF CANADA'S TWO OFFICIAL LANGUAGES, ENGLISH AND FRENCH

In your own words, explain to a partner what you think these rights mean. Are these rights promised everywhere in the world? Should they be?

B. Have a discussion in small groups. In Canada, capital punishment is illegal. It is legal in some other countries. What is your opinion: Should the death penalty exist for some crimes, or not at all? If so, which crimes do you think should carry the death penalty?

C. What can be done to make sure that courts convict only people who are guilty?

SNAPSHOT OF CANADA

- Between 1892 and 1961, the penalty for all murders in Canada was death by hanging—710 murderers were executed.
- In 1963, the death penalty was restricted to the murder of an on-duty police officer or prison guard.
- In 1976, capital punishment was abolished except for some military offences.
- In 1998, the death penalty was completely abolished.
- The last execution was carried out on December 11, 1962, when two men were hanged in Toronto, Ontario.

Unit Reflection
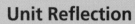

How have advances in technology helped or hindered crime-scene investigations?

ethics   the study of right and wrong or good and bad behaviou

DISCUSSION

1. Calvin thought carefully about the pros (for) and cons (against) of cheating on his test. Which argument in favour of cheating do you think is best? Which argument against cheating do you think is best? Why? Did Calvin behave in an ethical way? Give your reasons.

2. Think about the last time you were tempted to make an unethical choice, but chose to act ethically. What were the reasons for your ethical choice? Think about the last time you made an unethical choice. What were the reasons for the unethical choice?

3. What makes people do the right thing? What makes them do the wrong thing? Why is the choice sometimes difficult?

Reading

Before You Read

A. Take the quiz, and then compare your answers with two classmates' answers.

Copyright Quiz ©

How Much Do You Know about Copyright Law in Canada?

1. What is copyright?
   a) Copyright means "the right to copy." Only the owner of copyright, usually the person who created a work, has a right to copy it.
   b) Copyright means that "people have a right to copy" someone else's work as long as they pay for it.
   c) Copyright means "photocopying a book is not right." Copyright is the law.
2. What is included in copyright?
   a) books, music, and films, but not computer programs
   b) paintings, films, books, and music, but not photographs
   c) books, music, plays, and films, but not paintings
   d) music, films, photographs, and books, but not commonly known facts in an article
3. Copyright is an example of the legal protection of *intellectual property*. Check all examples of intellectual property that are protected by law.
   ☐ a) Trademarks™ (graphics), which distinguish the products or services of one company from those of another
   ☐ b) Patents, which protect new and useful inventions
   ☐ c) Methods, which include how something is done (e.g., manufacturing methods)
   ☐ d) Industrial designs—the original designs for a finished, manufactured product

4) In the privacy of your own home, things may be different. Check if each situation is legal or illegal.

Legal Illegal
☐ ☐ a) You give a private performance of someone else's song or play in your own home.
☐ ☐ b) You make a copy of a musical CD for private use.
☐ ☐ c) You make a copy of a DVD movie protected by copyright to watch only in your own home.
☐ ☐ d) You copy a chapter from a book for private study at home.

B. Do you think giving these legal protections for artists and creators of products and services is the right thing to do? Why?

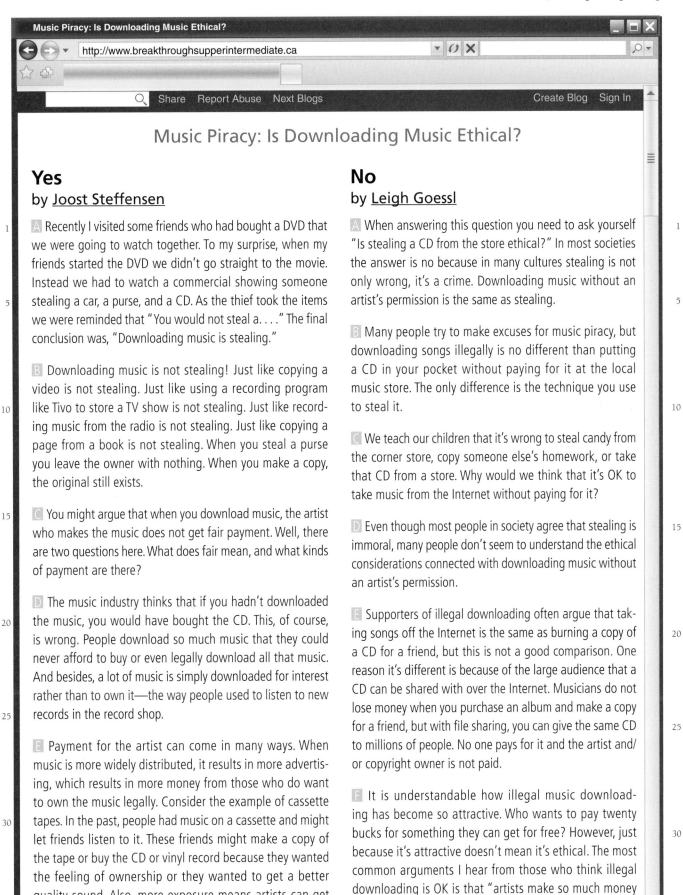

Music Piracy: Is Downloading Music Ethical?

http://www.breakthroughsupperintermediate.ca

Share   Report Abuse   Next Blogs   Create Blog   Sign In

Music Piracy: Is Downloading Music Ethical?

Yes
by Joost Steffensen

A Recently I visited some friends who had bought a DVD that we were going to watch together. To my surprise, when my friends started the DVD we didn't go straight to the movie. Instead we had to watch a commercial showing someone stealing a car, a purse, and a CD. As the thief took the items we were reminded that "You would not steal a. . . ." The final conclusion was, "Downloading music is stealing."

B Downloading music is not stealing! Just like copying a video is not stealing. Just like using a recording program like Tivo to store a TV show is not stealing. Just like recording music from the radio is not stealing. Just like copying a page from a book is not stealing. When you steal a purse you leave the owner with nothing. When you make a copy, the original still exists.

C You might argue that when you download music, the artist who makes the music does not get fair payment. Well, there are two questions here. What does fair mean, and what kinds of payment are there?

D The music industry thinks that if you hadn't downloaded the music, you would have bought the CD. This, of course, is wrong. People download so much music that they could never afford to buy or even legally download all that music. And besides, a lot of music is simply downloaded for interest rather than to own it—the way people used to listen to new records in the record shop.

E Payment for the artist can come in many ways. When music is more widely distributed, it results in more advertising, which results in more money from those who do want to own the music legally. Consider the example of cassette tapes. In the past, people had music on a cassette and might let friends listen to it. These friends might make a copy of the tape or buy the CD or vinyl record because they wanted the feeling of ownership or they wanted to get a better quality sound. Also, more exposure means artists can get more money by having their music used in advertising or movies.

(continued on next page)

No
by Leigh Goessl

A When answering this question you need to ask yourself "Is stealing a CD from the store ethical?" In most societies the answer is no because in many cultures stealing is not only wrong, it's a crime. Downloading music without an artist's permission is the same as stealing.

B Many people try to make excuses for music piracy, but downloading songs illegally is no different than putting a CD in your pocket without paying for it at the local music store. The only difference is the technique you use to steal it.

C We teach our children that it's wrong to steal candy from the corner store, copy someone else's homework, or take that CD from a store. Why would we think that it's OK to take music from the Internet without paying for it?

D Even though most people in society agree that stealing is immoral, many people don't seem to understand the ethical considerations connected with downloading music without an artist's permission.

E Supporters of illegal downloading often argue that taking songs off the Internet is the same as burning a copy of a CD for a friend, but this is not a good comparison. One reason it's different is because of the large audience that a CD can be shared with over the Internet. Musicians do not lose money when you purchase an album and make a copy for a friend, but with file sharing, you can give the same CD to millions of people. No one pays for it and the artist and/ or copyright owner is not paid.

F It is understandable how illegal music downloading has become so attractive. Who wants to pay twenty bucks for something they can get for free? However, just because it's attractive doesn't mean it's ethical. The most common arguments I hear from those who think illegal downloading is OK is that "artists make so much money anyway," and "that artist is making it about the money, not the music!"

(continued on next page)

Yes

F While watching the warning on my friends' DVD I couldn't believe the contradiction. Here I was watching something he owned, and he could not skip the warning or fast-forward past it. Every time he wanted to see the movie he legally owned, he was going to have to feel like a criminal.

G You have to wonder what the movie and music industries are thinking. They offer products that are more expensive and at the same time less convenient than free copies. It makes no sense.

H Then there is the issue that really upsets me: transferability. I own lots of cassette tapes. But I don't listen to tapes any more. I want to listen to that music on my computer. If the songs were on CD, I could simply copy them. But if I want them on my PC, I have to download the music. Now, by law, this is illegal. But I already paid the artist when I bought the tape. Why should I pay him or the industry again for something that costs them no more money?

I And it gets worse. If you buy a computer game, you have to pay for that game again for each type of equipment you want to play it on. If you want to play on your console, on your PC, and on your hand-held device, you have to pay three times. You have to even pay more often if you keep buying newer consoles.

J What if your computer crashes and you lose your songs? You have to buy them again. What does that have to do with intellectual property rights? Haven't you already paid for them?

K Basically, the music industry should get out of the distribution business and focus on rights management. Record companies should make songs available on the Internet and have people pay a few cents to buy the right to listen to a song for the rest of their lives. They could create a large database of the names of people who have bought the rights to a song. Once we buy the right to a song, it should be free in the future. If we somehow lose the music, we can download it again, for free. Oh, and of course if we can show we already have the tape, the CD, or the record, we should get the rights for free.

L Until then, the only way to force the music industry to improve products and make them consumer-friendly is simply to keep downloading. It's quicker, it's cheaper, and it's more fun.

No

G It's one thing if an artist creates a website and chooses to release music for free downloading, usually in the hopes that someone will like and buy the CD or go to one of their shows, but what about artists who don't want their music downloaded? Isn't it their right to control their intellectual property? Offering free downloads is a brilliant marketing tool for musicians, but the decision of whether or not to use that tool should be made by the person(s) who own the songs, not the Internet users who download them.

H CDs are indeed overpriced, and though the artists may be rich and have more money than they could possibly spend, the bottom line is the music is still an asset they created and it belongs to them. If an artist has not given permission for his or her music to be available for download, then downloading is theft, no matter what false arguments we use to make ourselves believe it's OK.

I Why is it so easy for people to commit this crime without feeling guilty? Is it because they don't have to face their victim? Or is it because they are not afraid that someone will see them commit the act? If the same crime was committed in a store, people would not feel so comfortable stealing.

J We live in a society where we can instantly satisfy our needs and wants. Downloading music is so quick and easy that there is little time to think about it. People quickly move onto the next thing in their lives without truly thinking about the consequences of their decision.

K Music piracy will continue to be a concern until those who steal music realize that just because it's easy to get something illegally doesn't mean it's ethical. Just because we *can* doesn't mean we *should*!

L Music piracy is morally wrong.

Internet   100%

Reading for Meaning

Write the letter of the paragraph(s) that correspond to each statement. Then, use your own words to write two or three sentences that explain the writers' views.

1. According to Steffensen, downloading music from the Internet without paying for it can actually benefit an artist. Explain.

2. Steffensen says the issue of transferability upsets him a lot. Explain.

3. In arguing against music piracy, Goessl raises a concern about intellectual property. Explain the concern.

4. According to Goessl, people who download music do not feel any guilt. Explain.

Reading for Similarities and Differences

Steffensen

Is it stealing? _____
Is it fair? _____
What should be done? _____
_____

Goessl

Is it stealing? _____
Is it fair? _____
What should be done? _____
_____

1. Both writers compare music piracy to stealing. How is downloading music from the Internet without paying for it similar to stealing? How is it different from stealing?

2. Is downloading music from the Internet without paying for it fair to the artist who created the music? Explain the reasons each writer gives for his or her views.

3. Music piracy is a concern (worry) for the music industry, many artists, and many Internet users. What does each writer think should happen to resolve this issue?

For Discussion

1. Steffensen argues that music piracy is ethical. In your opinion, what are his most and least persuasive arguments? Why?

2. Goessl argues that music piracy is unethical. In your opinion, what are her most and least persuasive arguments? Why?

3. Do not consider your personal opinion about the topic. Overall, who do you think makes the better arguments for his or her views? Why?

Thinking outside the Box

Is Something Missing?

A good opinion can only be formed after a person has thought about the many different aspects of a topic. What ideas about music piracy have the writers not considered?

Vocabulary

Exercise A

Circle the word that completes the sentence and has a similar meaning to the words in *italics*. Use your knowledge of word roots to help you.

1. You are *obligated to explain your actions and decisions to others*. You are . . .
   a) accountable   b) unethical   c) legal

2. Before you decide, consider the *effects* of your action. Consider the . . .
   a) fairness   b) consequences   c) value

3. The politician *uses her power to get personal benefits*. She lets business executives break the law if they pay her money. The politician is . . .
   a) corrupt   b) lying   c) trustworthy

4. Rules must *apply equally to everyone*. Therefore, punishing cheaters is . . .
   a) accountable   b) honest   c) fair

5. You feel bad because *you know you have done something wrong*. That is the feeling of . . .
   a) trustworthiness   b) guilt   c) value

6. My action didn't *hurt anyone*, so I don't think it was wrong. It wasn't . . .
   a) accountable   b) dishonest   c) harmful

7. It's not always good to be *truthful*. . . . is not always best.
   a) honesty   b) fairness   c) behaviour

8. He can be *depended on* to do the right thing. He is . . .
   a) corrupt   b) guilty   c) trustworthy

9. In Canada, uploading music to the Internet is against the law, but sharing music files is *allowed by the law*. Sharing music is . . .
   a) corrupt   b) unethical   c) legal

10. If my mother *doesn't tell the truth* about how old she is, is she acting unethically? Afterall, she is . . .
    a) accountable   b) corrupt   c) lying

11. Canadians think that freedom and equality are *important principles*. Freedom and equality are strong Canadian . . .
    a) values   b) ethics   c) consequences

12. In Canada, the law says you cannot *take someone's property without permission*. That's . . .
    a) stealing   b) lying   c) cheating

13. Your values influence *how you act*. They guide your . . .
    a) consequences   b) behaviour   c) accountability

14. The rules state that you cannot copy a classmate's test answers. Copying someone's answers is *breaking the rules*. That's . . .
    a) trustworthiness   b) cheating   c) guilt

Exercise B

Discuss each statement and decide if you agree or disagree. Try to get a group consensus.

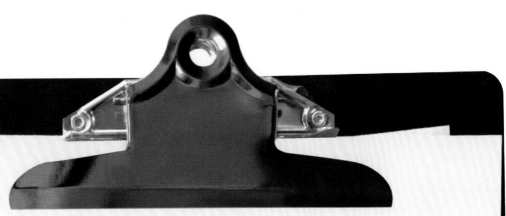

	Agree	Disagree
People will be less likely to lie$_1$, cheat$_2$, or steal$_3$ if they think no one will catch them.	○	○
Downloading music or movies from the Internet should be legal$_4$.	○	○
If students cheat on an assignment, they must accept the consequences$_5$—a grade of zero.	○	○
When one business is corrupt$_6$, it forces other businesses to be dishonest as well.	○	○
Politicians are more trustworthy$_7$ than business leaders because they are not motivated by making money.	○	○
An action is not unethical$_8$ unless it directly harms$_9$ someone.	○	○
People must be accountable$_{10}$ for their behaviour. They must be able to explain the reasons for their ethical choices.	○	○
It's important to know what your values$_{11}$ are because they guide your behaviour$_{12}$.	○	○
Most people value fairness$_{13}$ more than honesty$_{14}$.	○	○
Guilt$_{15}$ motivates people to do the right thing more than punishment does.	○	○

Exercise C

Use a dictionary. Write the different grammatical forms of the words to complete the chart.

Verb	Noun	Adjective
	accountability	
behave		
~~	(action) cheater (person)	~~~~~~ ~~~~~~ ~~~~~~
corrupt		consequential
~~	ethics	
~~		fair
~~	guilt	
		harmful
~~		honest
		legal
	lying (action)	
	liar (person)	
	stealing (action)	

Vocabulary in Use

Read the following situations. Each situation is an example of one (or more) of the ideas expressed in the words below. State what each situation is an example of. Be prepared to explain your choices.

accountability	illegality
cheating	legality
consequences	lying
corruption	stealing
fairness	trustworthiness
guilt	unfairness
harm	untrustworthiness
honesty	value

Example:

Situation: Jenny's brother told his parents he went to school today, but he really didn't.

Response: <u>This situation is an example of lying and/ or untrustworthiness.</u>

1. Frank knew it was wrong of him to take paper, pens, and other supplies from the office where he worked. He felt bad about it.

2. Jamie's friends liked him. If they told him their problems or told him a secret, he never told anyone else.

3. The government officials often accepted bribes (money) in return for closing their eyes to illegal activities.

4. In Ontario, people are not allowed by law to smoke in cars with young children because second-hand smoke hurts children.

5. Mike and Lisa always came fifteen to thirty minutes late to class. They did not have good reasons for arriving late. As a result, the teacher decided to make a new rule. Once class started, he locked the door and did not allow late students to enter the room.

6. The police officer stopped a speeding car to give the driver a ticket. The driver was driving thirty kilometres per hour over the speed limit. The driver gave the officer a hundred dollar bill. The officer took the cash and drove away. She did not give the driver a ticket.

7. Chris's parents paid for his wedding. They liked his new wife. A few years later Chris's sister got married. Chris's parents did not like her new husband, but they paid for her wedding too. They felt they had an obligation to treat their two children equally.

8. In Canada, people who work must tell the government how much money they have earned and pay tax on this money. This is the law. Ms. Linell works as a server in a restaurant. She told the government how much money the restaurant paid her last year, but she did not tell the government about all the money she earned in tips from her customers.

Grammar Focus

Exercise A

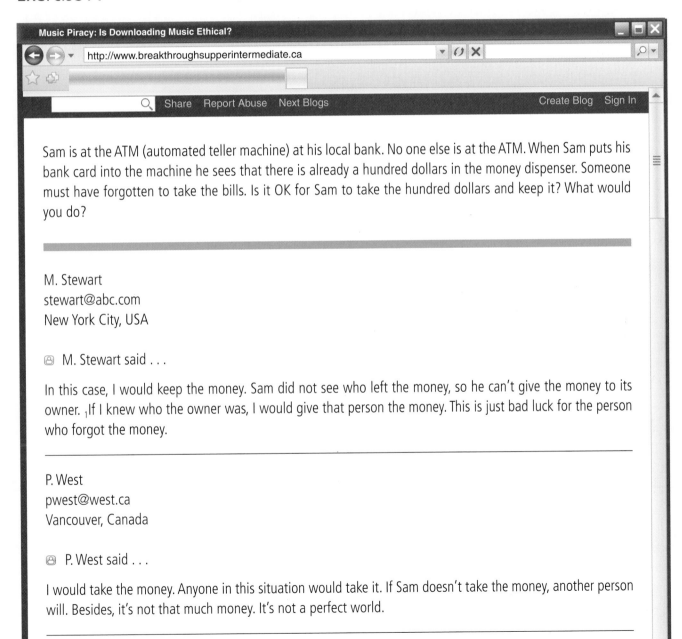

Music Piracy: Is Downloading Music Ethical?

http://www.breakthroughsupperintermediate.ca

Share   Report Abuse   Next Blogs   Create Blog   Sign In

Sam is at the ATM (automated teller machine) at his local bank. No one else is at the ATM. When Sam puts his bank card into the machine he sees that there is already a hundred dollars in the money dispenser. Someone must have forgotten to take the bills. Is it OK for Sam to take the hundred dollars and keep it? What would you do?

M. Stewart
stewart@abc.com
New York City, USA

M. Stewart said . . .

In this case, I would keep the money. Sam did not see who left the money, so he can't give the money to its owner. ₁If I knew who the owner was, I would give that person the money. This is just bad luck for the person who forgot the money.

P. West
pwest@west.ca
Vancouver, Canada

P. West said . . .

I would take the money. Anyone in this situation would take it. If Sam doesn't take the money, another person will. Besides, it's not that much money. It's not a perfect world.

C. Michaels
micha@soneyside.au
Brisbane, Australia

🔒 C. Michaels said . . .

I wouldn't keep the money and I don't think Sam should, either. I would take the money, go to the bank counter and leave it with an employee in case the rightful owner comes back. That's the right thing to do. If I forgot a hundred dollars at an ATM, I'd go back to see if the money was still there. I'd ask at the bank counter if someone had turned it in. There's a good chance the owner will return to see if the money is still there.

___

T. Laroche
tclaroche@citycable.ca
Montreal, Canada

🔒 T. Laroche said . . .

I would take the money, but I wouldn't keep it. Sam didn't earn the money. I think Sam should take the hundred dollars and donate it to a charity. That way something good would result from the owner's loss. He should donate the money the same day, though. If he doesn't do it right away, he'll forget about donating the money and keep it.

🌐 Internet   🔍 100% ▾

1. M. Stewart thinks that, in this situation, Sam should keep the money. What would have to be different in the situation for M. Stewart to advise Sam not to keep the money?

2. What prediction does P. West make?

3. Did C. Michaels ever forget a hundred dollars at an ATM machine? How do you know?

4. Why does T. Laroche think Sam should donate the money to a charity right away?

5. • *If* sentences have two parts. Underline the two parts of each *if* sentence in the boxes. What is the relationship between the two parts of an *if* sentence?

   • Read the sentences in Group A. Then, read the sentences in Group B. In one group, the situation of the *if* clauses is not possible given the facts of the story. Which group has the sentences whose conditions are impossible (not real)?

Group A

If I knew who the owner was, I would give that person the money.

If I forgot $100 at an ATM, I'd go back to see if the money was still there.

Group B

If Sam doesn't take the money, another person will.

If he doesn't do it right away, he'll forget about donating the money and keep it.

Conditional Sentences

a) *If* sentences show a condition/result relationship. If the condition is true, then the result will also be true.

Example:

If Sam doesn't take the money, another person will.

　　　　condition (if this happens)　　　result (then this will happen)

b) We distinguish between conditions that are possible or likely to be true and conditions that are impossible or unlikely to be true.

Example:

If he doesn't do it right away, he'll forget about donating the money and keep it.

　　　　　possible condition　　　　　　　　　　　result
(In this situation the condition is possible/likely. It can be true.)

If I knew who the owner was, I would give that person the money.

　　　　　impossible condition　　　　　　　　　result
(In this situation the condition is impossible. It is not true.)

Exercise B

Check if the condition is possible/likely (real) or impossible/unlikely (unreal). If it is unreal, state the reality.

	Possible	Impossible or unlikely
1. If you cheat on a test, you will get a grade of zero.	☐	☐
2. If you lie to your girlfriend, she will not trust you in the future.	☐	☐
3. People would not behave ethically if there were no laws.	☐	☐
4. If Tim thought he would not get caught, he might cheat on the exam.	☐	☐
5. If you break the law, you will be punished.	☐	☐
6. If my brother killed someone, I would lie for him.	☐	☐
7. The economy would be destroyed if all business leaders were corrupt.	☐	☐
8. Store security guards will stop you if they see you stealing.	☐	☐

- What do you notice about the position of the *if* clause in the sentences above? Does the meaning of the sentence change when the *if* clause is in a different position? If the *if* clause in the sentence is moved, is it necessary to make any other changes to the sentence?

- Real conditional sentences and unreal conditional sentences have different grammatical forms. What differences do you notice? Write out the grammatical form for each.

Real and Unreal Conditionals

In *if* sentences where the condition is possible or likely to happen, we use tenses in the same way as we do in other sentences.

Examples:

Situation: I'm thinking about lying to my parents about going out with Jim on a date. They don't want me to date, but I'm planning to go with friends, so what's the harm? I think my parents are being unreasonable. It's only a small lie, anyway.

Conditional: If I *lie* to my parents, they *won't know* that I'm dating Jim. (In this situation, it is possible that I will lie to them.)

Use the real conditional to show that there is a possibility that the condition will happen. Use tenses in the same way as in other sentences.

In unreal conditionals, the condition is impossible or not likely to happen. The condition is only in the speaker's imagination. To signal that the condition is unreal, we use a past tense form of the verb.

Examples:

Situation: I'm going to graduate from college soon. I have a B average. My parents might be a little disappointed in my grades. My friend suggested that I tell my parents I have an A+ average, but I don't intend to lie to them. Honesty is important to me.

Conditional: If I *lied* to my parents, I *would feel* guilty. (In this situation, it's highly unlikely I will lie to my parents. I'm just imagining it.)

Use the unreal conditional to show that you don't think the condition will happen. Put the verbs in the past tense to show that the actions are only imagined and not real.

Note: Use *were* instead of *was* in the unreal conditional.

Exercise C

What would you do in these imaginary situations? Fill in the blanks with a correct form of the verb.

1. If I _____ (see) a young boy stealing a toy in a store, I _____ (tell) him to put the toy back.

2. I'm not sure what I _____ (do) if I _____ (see) an elderly woman stealing food in a grocery store.

3. If a classmate _____ (try) to copy my test answers, I _____ (cover) my paper.

4. I _____ (be) very angry if a teacher _____ (insult) a student in class.

5. If my friend _____ (cheat) on her boyfriend, I _____ (tell) her boyfriend.

Pronunciation Power

A contraction is a shortened form of two words that are linked in a sentence. For example, rather than saying, "*He will* do the right thing," we can remove the first two letters of the word *will* and say, "*He'll* do the right thing." Similarly, we can reduce "*She would* tell the truth" to "*She'd* tell the truth." Using contractions to link words allows us to speak more rhythmically. Contractions are very common in spoken language and in informal writing.

Would / Wouldn't

Listen and repeat the sentences. Pay attention to the sound the contractions make.

would contractions (+verb)

I'd behave ethically.
You'd disappoint your parents.
He'd accept the consequences.
She'd feel guilty.

It'd be fair.
We'd be dishonest.
They'd be corrupt.

***would not* contractions (+verb)**

I wouldn't be honest.
You wouldn't cheat your business partner.
He wouldn't steal from his brother.
She wouldn't lie.
It wouldn't be fair.
We wouldn't feel guilty.
They wouldn't ask me to lie.

Exercise A

Check ✔ the recorded sentence you hear.

1. a) ☐ I feel guilty.
   b) ☐ I'd feel guilty.

2. a) ☐ He won't steal from his friend.
   b) ☐ He wouldn't steal from his friend.

3. a) ☐ It'd be fair.
   b) ☐ It wouldn't be fair.

4. a) ☐ You have to accept the consequences.
   b) ☐ You'd have to accept the consequences.

5. a) ☐ We'd lie for you.
   b) ☐ We wouldn't lie for you.

6. a) ☐ She'll do the right thing.
   b) ☐ She'd do the right thing.

7. a) ☐ They won't act ethically.
   b) ☐ They wouldn't act ethically.

8. a) ☐ It'd be dishonest.
   b) ☐ I'd be dishonest.

9. a) ☐ It'd be fair.
   b) ☐ It wouldn't be fair.

10. a) ☐ It'd be corrupt.
    b) ☐ I'd be corrupt.

Now take turns with a partner to practise your pronunciation. One partner will choose one sentence in each pair to read aloud while the other partner marks the sentence she or he hears.

Exercise B

Write the numbers 1 to 10 in the order in which you hear the sentences. The first one has been marked for you.

○ He wouldn't be OK.
○ He'd be OK.
○ I would be OK.
① I'd be OK.
○ I'll be OK.
○ It won't be OK.
○ It wouldn't be OK.
○ It'd be OK.
○ It'll be OK.
○ We'd be OK.

Now take turns with a partner to practise your pronunciation. One partner will choose an order in which to read the sentences aloud while the other partner marks the order of the sentences.

Grammar in Use

Interview a partner to learn more about his or her values. Take turns asking a question. Be prepared to share information about your partner with others in the class.

1. Under what conditions would you steal food?

2. Would you lie for a friend under any condition? Explain.

3. Would you ever break the law? Explain.

4. Are there any conditions under which it would be OK to lie to a spouse? Explain.

5. Are there any situations in which you think it is OK to kill another person?

Listening

Before You Listen

It is illegal and unethical to steal someone's property. In North American culture, a person's ideas and words are considered his or her intellectual property. In the same way that you cannot steal someone's watch or car, you cannot steal someone's words or ideas. If you copy someone's words or ideas without saying whose ideas they are and where you found the information, you are plagiarizing. Plagiarism can happen in professional and educational situations. Copyright laws protect a person from having their ideas and words stolen. Plagiarism is a crime.

1. Why do you think people plagiarize? List four or five reasons.
2. What are the benefits and disadvantages of treating ideas and words as property that a person can own?
3. Is plagiarism illegal in your first country? Why?
4. How common is plagiarism in schools in your home country? What are the consequences of plagiarism?

You will hear two conversations that deal with a case of plagiarism.

Part 1

Listening to Identify Context

a) Who are the conversation partners? What is their relationship?
b) What is the purpose of this conversation?
c) In your own words, explain the situation.

Listening for Specific Information

d) What evidence is there that the paper has been plagiarized? Give two pieces of evidence.
e) What advice is given?
f) What are the consequences of plagiarizing?

Part 2

Listening to Identify Context

a) Who are the conversation partners?
b) Why are these two people having this conversation?
c) In your own words, briefly explain the situation.

Comprehension Check

d) What did Gigi misunderstand about plagiarism?
e) Is it OK for Gigi to write *inflation stimulates business* without citing her source (telling where the information came from)? Why or why not?
f) Gigi gets advice. What should she do if she is not sure whether or not she needs to cite a source?

Listening for Specific Information

g) What are the five situations where you must cite your source?

For Discussion

1. Did Gigi really plagiarize? Why?
2. What do you think the teacher should do next? Why?
3. What do you think the teacher will do next? Why?

Thinking outside the Box

This story raises some important topics for discussion about plagiarism. The reading activity on pages 85–86 raised some important concerns about downloading music from the Internet. What similarities and differences are there between the two issues?

Writing

One way to avoid plagiarizing is to paraphrase. When we paraphrase, we communicate another writer's ideas, but we use our own words.

Exercise A

Work with a partner. Read and discuss the meaning of the sentences. Cover the original sentences so you are not tempted to copy them. Then, write the idea in your own words. You may write more than one sentence to express the full idea.

Example:
Laws about the sharing and downloading of music on the Internet vary from country to country.

Every country has . . . different laws about sharing and downloading music on the Internet.

1. According to Canadian law, downloading copyrighted music from peer-to-peer networks is legal, but uploading those files is not.
2. In Canada, consumers are charged a special fee when they buy recording products like blank CDs. The fee is included in the price of the product. These fees are used to fund musicians and songwriters for revenues lost due to consumer copying.
3. Canada allows a person to make copies of sound recordings for personal, non-commercial use.
4. According to US law, a person can go to prison for five years and have to pay up to $250,000 for downloading music illegally. This is true even if the downloaded material wasn't copied and distributed for financial or commercial gain.

Exercise B

When we paraphrase, we begin with a phrase of introduction that tells the reader whose idea it is, and then we use our own words to state the idea. The sentences below are direct quotes about ethics. Paraphrase each idea using one of the expressions below. Remember to focus on the writer's main idea, not the structure of the original sentence.

…says that	…believes that	…argues that
…thinks that	According to…,	…claims that

Example:
"If you create something and then someone takes it without your permission, that is stealing."
—Mary J. Blige, American recording artist, songwriter, singer, and actress

• Mary J. Blige argues that you are stealing if you take something that someone creates without their permission.
• According to Mary J. Blige, if you take something that someone creates without their permission, you are stealing.

1. "Falsehood is so easy, truth so difficult."
   —George Elliot (1819–1880), English novelist
2. "Never do anything against conscience, even if the state [government] demands it."
   —Albert Einstein (1879–1955), German-born American physicist
3. "Right is right, even if everyone is against it; and wrong is wrong, even if everyone is for it."
   —William Penn (1644–1718), English real estate entrepreneur and philosopher
4. "Good people do not need laws to tell them to act responsibly, while bad people will find a way around the laws."
   —Plato (428/427–348/347 BCE), Greek philosopher and mathematician
5. "What you do not wish for yourself, do not do to others."
   —Confucius (K'ung-tzu) (551–479 BCE), Chinese thinker and social philosopher

Exercise C

Another way to avoid plagiarizing is to use a direct quotation. A quotation uses the exact words of the writer or speaker.

• Begin a direct quotation with a phrase of introduction like the ones in Exercise B.
  Note: We often remove the word *that*.
• Put a comma after the phrase of introduction.
• Use open quotation marks at the start of the sentence(s) and closing quotation marks after it.

Example:

Steffensen argues, "When music is more widely distributed, it results in more advertising, which results in more money from those who do want to own the music legally."

Note: The closing quotation mark comes after the sentence punctuation of the original sentence.

Read the following paraphrased ideas. Find the exact words in the reading on pages 85–86 and write the quoted sentence as in the example. You may need to quote more than one sentence to communicate the full idea. Use different phrases of introduction.

1. (Yes, Par. B) Steffensen claims that downloading music and stealing are not the same thing.
2. (Yes, Par. K) According to Steffensen, the music industry should stop distributing music and should manage people's rights to own music instead.
3. (No, Par. H) Goessl believes that downloading music without the artist's permission is stealing and there are no good reasons for doing it.
4. (No, Par. E) Goessl says that musicians don't lose money when you give a copy of a CD that you bought to a friend, but they do lose money when you share a copy with a million other people through the Internet.

Exercise D

Music piracy: Is downloading music from the Internet ethical? Write a paragraph stating your opinion. Include two ideas from the reading on pages 85–86 in your paragraph. Use a direct quotation or paraphrase.

Speaking

1. Values are the beliefs we have about what is important in life. We make decisions about what is right and wrong based on our values.
   a) Think about some important ethical decisions you have made in your life. Check ☑ the five values that have been most important in guiding you to make these decisions.

   ☐ A person should act for the good of the society first and for their personal desires last.

   ☐ All people must obey the law, regardless of their status in society.

   ☐ Equality is important.

   ☐ Keeping harmony within the group is important.

   ☐ Loyalty to family is important.

   ☐ People must be held accountable for their actions.

   ☐ People must be treated fairly.

   ☐ People should be kind to others.

   ☐ People should be tolerant of beliefs and behaviours that are different from their own.

   b) Check with your classmates to see which values they have found most important. Are your values similar or different? Discuss the reasons for your choices.

2. Work in small groups. Discuss the ethics of the following situations. Be prepared to share a summary of your group discussion with the whole class.

   a) Sally has been offered a job by a company that she knows exploits child labour in a developing country to make its products. Should she take the job? Explain.

   b) Karel is applying to attend a university in Canada. The application form requires him to list all his previous education. Karel attended university in his home country, but failed his program and did not get a degree. He does not list this experience on his application form. Has Karel behaved ethically? Explain.

   c) Frank has a summer job at a movie theatre. He discovers that some of his co-workers are letting their friends in to see movies for free. Should he report this to the management? Explain.

SNAPSHOT OF CANADA

The Canadian Human Rights Act and provincial human rights laws legally protect Canadians from discrimination based on race, national or ethnic origin, colour, religion, age, sex, marital status, family status, pardoned conviction, disability, and sexual orientation. People working in organizations such as schools, retail stores, restaurants, and factories are protected by provincial human rights laws. Provincial human rights laws also make discrimination in housing illegal: for example, you cannot refuse to rent an apartment to someone because of that person's race or religion.

Unit Reflection

It can be difficult to make good ethical decisions. Look at the list of common traps that people fall into when they make ethical decisions. These are examples of poor logic. Discuss the meaning of each trap. Then, look through this unit to find three or four examples of thinking based on these traps.

Common Traps

- If it's necessary, it's ethical.
- If it's legal, it's OK.
- I'm just fighting fire with fire. They deserve it if I do something unethical.
- It doesn't hurt anyone, so it's OK.
- Everyone's doing it, so it's OK for me to do it too, even if it's unethical.
- It's OK to do it if I don't benefit personally.
- I didn't know it was unethical, so it was OK.

Love is imagined perfect life, but marriage is real life. Therefore, love and marriage are not the same thing.

When you are in love, you may not see things clearly. In marriage, however, romantic love begins to fade and you begin to see clearly again.

In a good marriage, partners must grow as one couple, but also as two individual people.

A successful marriage is based on friendship.

Young women are making a mistake if they think they can change their husbands.

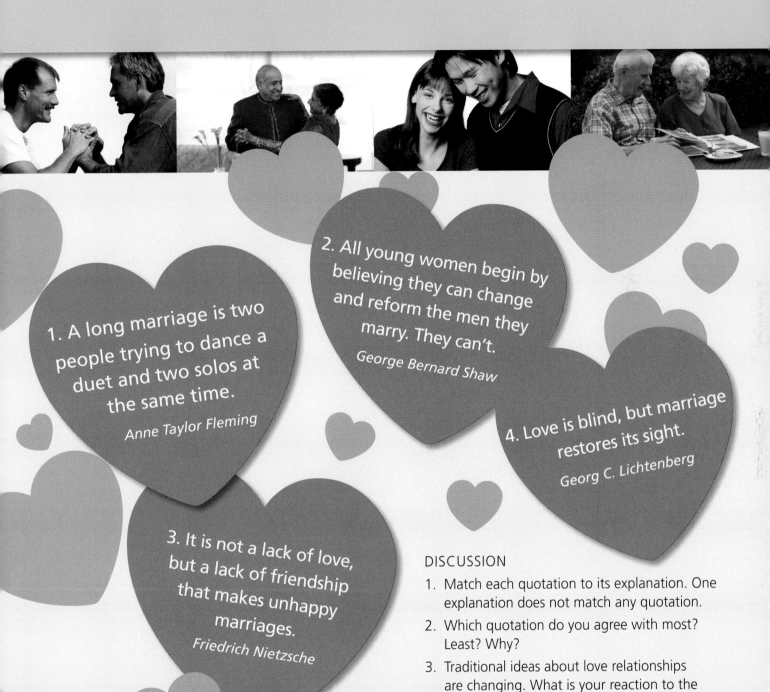

1. A long marriage is two people trying to dance a duet and two solos at the same time.

Anne Taylor Fleming

2. All young women begin by believing they can change and reform the men they marry. They can't.

George Bernard Shaw

4. Love is blind, but marriage restores its sight.

Georg C. Lichtenberg

3. It is not a lack of love, but a lack of friendship that makes unhappy marriages.

Friedrich Nietzsche

DISCUSSION

1. Match each quotation to its explanation. One explanation does not match any quotation.

2. Which quotation do you agree with most? Least? Why?

3. Traditional ideas about love relationships are changing. What is your reaction to the photos of the couples on these pages? What are the advantages and disadvantages of traditional ideas about love relationships and couples?

Reading

Marriage customs differ around the world. In some cultures, families arrange for their sons' and daughters' marriages. In some cases, families ask if the son or daughter agrees to the marriage. In other cases, the marriage is arranged without the agreement of the son or daughter. These kinds of marriages are called *arranged marriages*. In other societies, arranged marriages are not common practice. Sons and daughters find partners and make the decision to marry by themselves. In some cases, the couple asks if the parents agree with the marriage. In other cases, they do not. These kinds of marriages are called *love marriages*. In Canada, the law says that two men or two women can also marry legally. One difference between arranged marriages and love marriages is that in a love marriage, love is expected to develop before marriage. In an arranged marriage, love is expected to develop after marriage.

Before You Read

A. People have different opinions about whether love marriages or arranged marriages are better. What are your views? Read each statement and check how strongly you agree or disagree.

	Strongly Agree	Agree	Disagree	Strongly Disagree
1. A marriage cannot be successful without love.	☐	☐	☐	☐
2. Love is not enough to have a successful marriage.	☐	☐	☐	☐
3. Arranged marriages disadvantage women more than men.	☐	☐	☐	☐
4. Love eventually disappears in all marriages, so you do not need to be in love before you marry.	☐	☐	☐	☐
5. Arranged marriages result in fewer divorces.	☐	☐	☐	☐
6. Arranged marriages are mainly designed to maintain a family's economic and social status.	☐	☐	☐	☐
7. Love marriages set up unrealistic expectations for both partners.	☐	☐	☐	☐
8. It doesn't matter whether you have an arranged marriage or a love marriage. The results are the same.	☐	☐	☐	☐

B. You will find these words and phrases in the reading. Check the box with the best definition for the word.

1. tradition
   a) ☐ a behaviour or belief that a group has had for a long time
   b) ☐ a behaviour or belief that a group thinks is good

2. passionate
   a) ☐ with strong emotion
   b) ☐ sexual

3. consulted
   a) ☐ thought about carefully
   b) ☐ asked for advice

4. appropriate
   a) ☐ good
   b) ☐ bad

5. astrology
   a) ☐ the study of the position of the stars and planets to predict the future
   b) ☐ the scientific study of the stars and planets

6. commitment
   a) ☐ promise to support each other
   b) ☐ disagreement

7. evidence
   a) ☐ information that shows something must be true or not true
   b) ☐ logical conclusion

8. purpose
    a) ☐ goal
    b) ☐ explanation

9. extended relations
    a) ☐ a relationship that lasts a long time
    b) ☐ family, including aunts, uncles, cousins, grandparents, etc.

10. uniting people
    a) ☐ breaking people apart
    b) ☐ bringing people together

11. blend
    a) ☐ mix; put together
    b) ☐ solve problems

12. spouse
    a) ☐ the person you are married to
    b) ☐ a husband's parent

On Love and Marriage: The East and West in All of Us

By Anand Ram

Growing up in a traditional Indian family and living in the West, in my experience, leads to one big ball of questions. First, to say that something is traditionally Indian means nothing. In fact, tradition is whatever
5 the family chooses—and each family is different. Sure, there may be some common Indian traditions, but how those traditions are followed shows the real differences between families. In fact, each family is so unique in the way it chooses to keep its traditions, that non-tradition
10 becomes the tradition. But I'm getting off topic.

Growing up in an Indian family in the West leads to a big ball of questions. Why do I say that? I could write a long essay to answer that, but I will focus on the one thing that has confused me the most: the idea
15 of love and marriage.

As a young boy I never admitted to wanting love, but I secretly wanted it in some way. When I was a

child, my understanding of love came from television, books and movies. Love was a magnificent thing in
20 the fictional world, giving normal people the power to do extraordinary things. In love stories, every puzzle piece eventually found where it rightly fit. It might interest you that I say I first learned about love from these sources, and not from my parents. That is
25 because my parents taught me about marriage, not love.

fictional: not real; in the imagination only
puzzle: pieces that fit together only one
    correct way.
source: the place something comes from

But there was a problem. Why was the connection between romantic love and marriage so clear in the world of books and movies, but not in my parents'
30 world? As I got older, I realized that the fictional world showed only one kind of love: passionate love, the kind of love that makes a great story, but not a great reality. When I looked at my parents' marriage, though, I started to see that there were different kinds
35 of love.

My parents' marriage was arranged, but not in the way some Westerners may imagine. I think Westerners commonly believe that arranged marriage happens when parents promise their sons and daughters to
40 each other's families at a very young age. This was not

the case with my own parents. When my father was twenty-six, he heard that my mother was "looking" for a husband, so he consulted his father. Twenty-six was considered an appropriate age for a man to marry. After
45 deliberating, through methods involving family analysis, education, and even astrology, my father asked my mother's father for her hand in marriage. My mother's family agreed, as did my mother, who was only nineteen at the time, and the wedding plans began.

deliberating: thinking about something carefully
her hand in marriage: permission to marry her

50 When I first heard this story, I could not understand the idea of an arranged marriage. My parents told me that this was just the way it was for them, and that "our culture" did not believe in this frivolous thing called *love.* Marriage was more about a commitment
55 between families than about what the man and woman wanted. To a young child who didn't question his parents, I thought they had pretty good evidence that love was frivolous and not a good basis for marriage. They pointed to the West and said, "Look, they believe in
60 divorce and 50 percent of all marriages here end in it." Their argument was that passionate love gets weaker with time and when it does, people get divorced. If a marriage is based primarily on romantic love, then when that fades, there's no reason to stay married.
65 Meanwhile, back home—home to them— marriages were built on economic, religious, and social commitments between families. These commitments do not diminish over time. In fact, they become stronger as the family has children and parents and grandparents
70 get older, so they do not believe in divorce. Arranged marriages made sense to them.

Fast-forward to me as a teenager with hormones blazing, and you see my confusion. I daydreamed about a romantic love partner, but I also wanted a
75 realistic marriage partner, and the two were not the same. In all honesty, I believed that a girl who was Indian, Hindu, and vegetarian was my "ideal" marriage partner. Any girl who did not fit this image was like a forbidden fruit. This, along with the rule that
80 I could not date until I was finished with my education and looking to get married, resulted in one very confused teen!

frivolous: not important; silly
hormones blazing: strong feelings as a result of developing sexual maturity
forbidden fruit: something you are not allowed to have

I asked the questions that were natural for someone caught between two cultures: Why did love and mar-
85 riage seem so far apart? Why didn't "we" believe in this idea of romantic love? Why couldn't I enjoy the company of the girls that made me feel happy on more than a friendly level? As I grew older, the questions began to get more difficult. What purpose did it serve on this
90 side of the world, far away from extended relations, to join two families by marriage? What was the point of committing your life to someone who didn't even know you? Why couldn't I be the one to finally make Indian marriage and passionate love make sense together?

95 Today I realize that these questions came from the rebellious attitude that many teenagers have. My parents' ideas about love and marriage restricted me in some ways, and I wanted to challenge their ideas. Eastern marriage was a contradiction. I thought that I was in a better position to
100 answer those questions, but as I grew out of adolescence into adulthood, I realized this was not true. First of all, I think I was asking the wrong questions. I assumed that romantic love did not have any place in Eastern marriages, but that isn't true. There *is* passion in those marriages; it's
105 just expressed in ways that I couldn't understand when I was younger. For example, my mother would not eat dinner before my father came home from work even when he came home very late. My parents used to kid around with each other all the time too, just like adolescents do
110 to hide their attraction to each other. At the time I didn't realize that these were expressions of love. Today, I am no longer willing to question a method of uniting people that has worked for this part of the world for so long (and continues to do so).

restricted: limited or controlled in your movements or actions
rebellious: fighting against the rules
contradiction: something that doesn't seem logical because it has opposite ideas
assumed: thought something was true without knowing if it was really true

Still, I do not think my adolescent questions were useless. As the son of immigrants, I had a Western mentality, but I also had knowledge of Eastern traditions and values. Asking these questions helped me to realize that I would have to find a way to balance Eastern and Western ways. There are some things about how I live my life that my parents may not understand, but I am committed to making an effort to understand how they live theirs.

So what will I do differently? How will I blend these two worlds? I will not accept an arranged marriage, but I will respect the idea that two families come together in marriage. I like the Western idea of dating because I think it is healthy to explore the attraction between two people. My parents may not agree, but I can approach the matter responsibly by being honest with them. It may result in fights and arguments, but my life is worth that.

When looking to the future, I want what I hope everyone wants, regardless of the culture in which they are raised. I want my spouse's family and my own to come together to share old traditions and begin new ones. I want us to understand the values and beliefs of each other's families, while at the same time developing our own values as a new family. I want passionate, romantic love, and I want it to last, but I also want a commitment based in mutual respect and I want that to last, too—for a lifetime.

---

balance: give the same value to
approach the matter: deal with or take an attitude
      toward the topic that is being discussed

Reading for the Main Idea

Circle the number of the sentence that best expresses the main idea.

1. Love marriages are better than arranged marriages.
2. It is possible to balance Eastern and Western ideas of marriage.
3. Young people need to live their own lives even if their parents do not agree with their choices.
4. Romantic love is not realistic.
5. Questioning your parents' values is disrespectful.

Reading for Meaning

Find the statement in the text and read a few sentences before and after the statement to understand its meaning. Then, for each statement, choose the one meaning that does NOT fit.

1. Growing up in an Indian family in the West leads to a big ball of questions. (*Lines 11–12*)
   a) Growing up in the West but in a family with Eastern traditions and values leads to confusion.
   b) When children grow up in Western culture but have parents who have Eastern values and traditions, it can be confusing for the children.
   c) The West is confused by Eastern values and traditions.
   d) Indian culture and Western culture have some different traditions and values. This can cause confusion for children of immigrants from India who grow up in the West.

2. In love stories, every puzzle piece eventually found where it rightly fit. (*Lines 21–22*)
   a) Things always work out well in love stories.
   b) Love always wins in love stories.
   c) Every love problem is fixed in love stories.
   d) In love stories, life is always confusing.

3. After deliberating, through methods involving family analysis, education, and even astrology, my father asked my mother's father for her hand in marriage. (*Lines 43–45*)
   a) First, my father carefully considered if it would be good to marry my mother. Then he asked my mother's father if he could marry her.
   b) Before my father asked my grandfather if he could marry my mother, he asked himself these questions: Was my mother's family a good family? Did my mother's education match his education? Did the position of the stars predict a good future for their marriage?
   c) There were many things to consider before asking for my mother's hand in marriage. Was she from a good family? Did she have a suitable education? Did the stars predict a good marriage for them?
   d) My father could not make the decision to marry my mother by himself. He had to consult his own father first.

4. If a marriage is based primarily on romantic love, then when that fades, there's no reason to stay married. (Lines 61–63)

   a) Romantic love does not exist in real life. Marriage is real life. Therefore, if you marry for romantic love, your marriage will not be a real marriage.

   b) If a couple marries for passion, then when passion dies the couple will not have a reason to stay married.

   c) Romantic love does not last. If people marry because of romantic love, they will have a reason to get divorced when the romance dies.

   d) If your main reason to get married is love, then your marriage will be in trouble. The kind of love people feel before they get married will not last. When they do not feel that same kind of love anymore, they have no reason to stay married.

5. I daydreamed about a romantic love partner, but I also wanted a realistic marriage partner, and the two were not the same. (Lines 71–74)

   a) In my dreams I would love someone, but I knew that in real life I could not marry that person.

   b) I always knew that my own marriage would be romantic.

   c) In my mind, love was something for my imagination, but marriage was something to think about in a real way.

   d) Love and marriage were two separate things. I dreamed about love, but I planned for marriage.

6. Why couldn't I enjoy the company of the people that made me feel happy on more than a friendly level? (Lines 84–86)

   a) Why was I not allowed to be with someone whom I liked romantically?

   b) Why was it not acceptable to be with people whom I was physically attracted to?

   c) Why did I only feel happy with friends?

   d) Why did I have to stay away from people I was attracted to in a romantic way?

7. Today, I am no longer willing to question a method of uniting people that has worked for this part of the world for so long (and continues to do so). (Lines 109–112)

   a) I am not going to question arranged marriage in India because it has worked, and still works, there.

   b) I am not going to ask any more questions about love and marriage. It takes too long.

   c) I will no longer challenge how people choose a marriage partner in India. It seems to have worked for them—and it still does.

   d) Arranged marriage has existed for a long time in Eastern culture and I don't think I should question the tradition there.

8. My parents may not agree, but I can approach the matter responsibly by being honest with them. (Lines 127–129)

   a) If my parents don't agree, I will respond by lying to them.

   b) My parents may not agree with my decisions, but I don't want to lie to them.

   c) Even if my parents don't agree, I will not lie to them.

   d) I want to be a responsible person, so I will not lie to my parents even if they don't agree with me.

Thinking outside the Box

Go back to the survey in the Before You Read section. Based on your understanding of the reading, answer the questions the way you think the writer would answer them. Compare your guesses to those of two or three classmates. Discuss any differences and explain your choices.

SNAPSHOT OF CANADA 📷

- Every province in Canada, except Quebec, requires that a couple be eighteen in order to marry without their parents' permission. In British Columbia, a couple has to be nineteen.
- Many people live together in common-law relationships without an official marriage document. In all provinces, except Quebec, after a period of time, common-law couples receive the same legal status as other married couples. There is no such thing as "common-law divorce."
- Same-sex marriages are legal in Canada.

Writing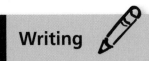

You receive the following email from a friend who has moved to Ireland. Write a response.

Subject: New Love

Dear _____,

Thanks for your last email. I'm glad things are going well for you.

   I love Ireland. The school where I'm studying is great and the Irish are very welcoming. I've taken a new English name. It's Jo. I'm making new friends from all over the world. It's all wonderful except for one little problem. I need your advice.

   I've fallen in love with someone from another country. I've told my parents, but they don't approve. They think that falling in love with someone who is not from our country is not good for me. They have forbidden me to date this person. I know it would be easy for me to see this person without my parents' knowledge. I don't want to hurt my parents, but I really love this person. You're my best friend—what do you think?

Jo
Btw, please don't tell anyone about my problem.

Vocabulary

Qualities of a partner

to be . . .	to have . . .
caring	a sense of humour
controlling	
honest	
jealous	
mature	
manipulative	
obsessive	
outgoing	
reliable	
respectful	
responsible	
stubborn	
trustworthy	

Exercise A

Not all of the words and phrases in the box are positive qualities of a person. Write the words in the appropriate column in the chart.

☺   ☹

_____   _____
_____   _____
_____   _____
_____   _____
_____   _____
_____   _____
_____

Exercise B

The words in Column B express the opposite of the words in Column A. Match the word with its opposite. In some cases, adding a prefix creates a word with the opposite meaning.

Column A	Column B
1. caring	a) dishonest
2. honest	b) trusting
3. jealous	c) shy
4. mature	d) unreliable
5. outgoing	e) flexible
6. reliable	f) immature
7. respectful	g) untrustworthy
8. responsible	h) selfish
9. stubborn	i) irresponsible
10. trustworthy	j) disrespectful

Exercise C

Read the following descriptions of people. Complete the sentences using the vocabulary in Exercise A. You will need to provide a verb in each case. More than one answer may be possible.

1. Even though Elisha is only fifteen, he's sensible and makes good judgments like an adult. I love that about him. Elisha _____.

2. I'm convinced that Phil would never do anything to harm me. I'm so comfortable around him. He has earned my respect. Phil _____.

3. I know Chris doesn't come across as a funny guy, but he has an amazing ability to see what's funny in situations and he has everyone laughing all the time. Chris _____.

4. I like that Paul never tells a lie. He's such a good person. Paul _____.

5. I love my brother. He's very kind and helpful. He's going to be a wonderful father one day. My brother _____.

6. I think there's something wrong with Lisa. When she gets something in her head, that's all she thinks about. She focuses on that one thing only and can't think about anything else. I don't think that's normal. Lisa _____.

7. I thought persistence was a good thing, but Emma is so persistent that it's a bad thing. She will not change her mind about anything, no matter how much you reason with her. She won't change her habits, either. It's becoming a problem in our relationship. Emma _____.

8. I'm afraid my mom was right about Adam. He plays mind games. He's always trying to force other people to do what he wants, and he does it in a way that the other person doesn't realize it. Adam _____.

9. It is a mistake for me to keep dating Jeremy. He doesn't trust me. Whenever I'm out with friends, he gets angry, especially if I'm out with my guy friends. He says he's just trying to protect me, but he acts like he owns me. I don't like it. Jeremy _____.

10. My parents adore Melissa. She's very polite and she always behaves in a way that shows them that she cares about them and that they're important to her. She's like that with everyone. Melissa _____.

11. Sam is driving me crazy. I think I have to break up with him. He's always telling me what to do and he wants to have power over me. I have no freedom at all. Sam _____.

12. Stephanie is so sociable. She loves to meet new people. She just likes being with other people. I really like that about her. Stephanie _____.

13. The best thing about Marta is that you can always depend on her. If she says she's going to do something, she'll do it. Marta _____.

14. A lot of people think young guys act like little boys and don't take their obligations seriously. Jim isn't like that all. He has excellent judgment, so he makes good decisions. And, if he makes a mistake, he doesn't try to blame it on someone else. Jim _____.

Vocabulary in Use

List the five most important qualities you look for in a boyfriend or girlfriend. Number them in order of importance. Then, list the five most important qualities you look for in a marriage partner. Number them in order of importance.

Compare your choices with classmates' choices.

- Are there differences between what people look for in a boyfriend or girlfriend and a marriage partner? Why?

- Collect the top three qualities for a marriage partner listed by the people in the class.
- Are there any patterns of differences in answers between the genders? Discuss the possible reasons.

Listening

Before You Listen

Complete the survey. Compare your results with a partner's. Give reasons for your opinions.

	Strongly Agree	*Agree*	*Disagree*	*Strongly Disagree*
1. It is possible to fall in love with someone the first time you meet.	○	○	○	●
2. A person can know within five to ten minutes of meeting someone if they'd like to date the person.	○	○	○	●
3. People should only date those whom they know well.	○	○	○	●
4. Dates that are organized by a company are safer than dates people arrange themselves.	○	○	○	●
5. People today cannot rely on traditional ways to meet possible partners.	○	○	○	●

Listening for Specific Information

Linda, Betty, and Lili are friends and co-workers. Listen to their conversation after work one day. Linda has some interesting news to share with her friends.

A. Listen to Excerpt 1: What is speed dating and how does it work?
B. Listen to Excerpt 2: Take point form notes. List at least three to four points of information for Paulo and three to four points of information for Linda.

Paulo	**Linda**
- 24 years old	- new to Vancouver
-	-
-	-
-	-
-	

Thinking outside the Box

Linda and Paulo's speed date lasted only five minutes. Based on the information you know about each of them, imagine their conversation. Work with a partner to write a short dialogue of ten to fifteen speaking turns.

Example:

Linda: Hi, my name is Linda.
Paulo: Hello, I'm Paulo.

Grammar Focus

Exercise A

Check your preference for each set of statements. Chose only ONE statement in each set. Share your preferences with a partner. Explain your choices.

1. a) ☐ I want someone *who just wants to have fun.*
   b) ☐ I'm interested in someone *who wants a serious relationship.*
2. a) ☐ I prefer someone *who is extroverted (outgoing).*
   b) ☐ I prefer someone *who is introverted (reflective).*
3. a) ☐ I want a relationship *that will lead to marriage.*
   b) ☐ I want a relationship *that is relaxed and easy-going.*
4. a) ☐ I want a date *that is exciting.*
   b) ☐ I want a date *that is romantic.*
5. a) ☐ I'm interested in movies *that are romantic.*
   b) ☐ I'm interested in movies *that have a lot of action.*

- What is the job of the part of the sentence in *italics*?

Exercise B

Draw a line to match the beginning of the sentence in Column A with the correct ending in Column B.

Column A	Column B
1. She doesn't want a partner	a) that expresses your love.
2. Trust and friendship build relationships	b) who has a good education.
3. It's always romantic to give a gift	c) that has a lot of violence.
4. Women like men	d) that is romantic.
5. On your first date, don't go to a movie	e) that will last forever.
6. He's looking for a partner	f) who is controlling.
7. Most people want marriages	g) that last.
8. Most couples want to go on a honeymoon	h) who treat them with respect.

Exercise C

1. Highlight the complete object in each sentence in Exercise A.
2. Each sentence contains an independent clause and a dependent clause.
   a) Highlight the independent clause.
   b) Underline the dependent clause.
   c) Identify the subject and verb of each dependent clause.
3. Identify which subject pronoun in each dependent clause refers to people and which refers to things.

Adjective Clause

A. We can describe a person, thing, idea, or place (noun) by adding a single adjective or a clause that behaves like an adjective.

Examples:

1. Adjective: She wants a **generous** man.
   Adjective clause: She wants a man **who is generous**.

   Both the adjective and adjective clause describe the noun *man* (person).

2. Adjective: He sent her a **romantic** card.
   Adjective clause: He sent her a card **that was romantic**.

   Both the adjective and adjective clause describe the noun *card* (thing).

B. An adjective clause follows the noun it describes.

1. Use **who** to introduce an adjective clause that describes people. **Who** is the subject of the adjective clause.

Example:

Sheila wants *a man* **who** has   a sense of humour.
        subject + verb   +   object
             _____
                adjective clause

2. Use **that** to introduce adjective clauses that describe things and ideas. **That** is the subject of the adjective clause.

Example:

They want *a honeymoon* **that** is exciting.
           subject + verb + adjective
             _____
                  adjective clause

Note: You can also use *that* to introduce an adjective clause that describes a person.

Exercise D

Use adjective clauses to combine the following sentences.

1. She married a man. The man has many good qualities.
2. I know many couples. The couples are happy in their marriages.
3. One of my friends went on a date. The date was unbelievably exciting.

4. They went on a honeymoon. The honeymoon was very romantic.
5. Her parents want her to date a man. He should not be much older than her.

Grammar in Use

When choosing a life partner, people should consider what kind of person will help them to achieve their goals in life and live the kind of life they want to live. Here is an exercise to help you think about what kind of partner suits you best.

1. Indicate your personal goals by writing two or three sentences for each category.
   a) I want a home *that . . . is big*.
   b) I want an education *that . . .*
   c) I want a job *that . . .*
   d) I want friends *who . . .*
   e) I want a lifestyle *that . . .*
   f) I want a family life *that . . .*

2. List eight to ten of your positive personal traits (personality and behavioural). Be honest.

   Example: I'm ambitious.

3. Review the list of your positive traits and your goals. You should choose a partner who brings out your best qualities and who shares your goals or can help you achieve them. Make a list of the five or six most important qualities, behaviours, and goals your life partner will need to have in order for you to achieve your goals. These are things you cannot live without. Be realistic.

   Example: I need a partner who wants children.

4. Make a list of five or six qualities and behaviours that you definitely do not want in a partner. These are traits that will kill the relationship. Remember to consider your own goals and personal traits.

   Example: I don't want a partner who is violent.

5. Prepare and practise saying five sentences that explain what kind of partner you are looking for and why. Be prepared to share your statements with the class.

   Example: I am looking for a partner who wants children because I want a big family.

Writing

Many singles use online dating services where they can search for a partner according to criteria such as age and religion. Members post a profile, which describes who they are and what they're looking for in a partner. The goal of a dating profile is to get the reader to take action—to send you an email and set up a date.

Imagine that you are single and looking for a partner. A friend has convinced you to join an online dating service.

1. Use the checklist below to write a profile like the one in the example. Think about your goals and your personal traits, likes, and dislikes. Decide whether you're looking for a fun, relaxed relationship or something more serious.

Checklist

An effective profile

☐ attracts attention in the headline. It is interesting to read.

☐ is written in a friendly style. It has no spelling or grammatical mistakes.

☐ describes the writer in a positive and unique way without exaggerating. It lets the reader know that the writer is different from the thousands of other people who are competing for a partner.

☐ describes in specific terms what the writer is looking for in a partner.

2. Share your profile with a classmate and discuss what makes each of your profiles appealing. Think of ways to make the profiles even more enticing.

If I Like You…Can I Keep You?

I am secure and happy with myself, but . . . life is meant for two! A little bit about myself: I enjoy travelling, camping by a lake, gardening, home decorating, going to comedy clubs and dinner theatre, listening to music, playing with my dog, and celebrating special occasions. I am self-sufficient, independent, and honest. I have a great sense of humour, and family and friends are very important to me. A man who has eyes ONLY for me and can make me laugh are important qualities! No pressure! Let's just relax . . . become friends and get to know each other . . . and see what happens.

Pronunciation Power

English has some common patterns for the rising and falling level of the voice in statements and questions. This rising and falling pattern is called *intonation*. The intonation pattern for the end of *wh–* (information) questions is different than for *yes/no* questions.

The voice level rises at the end of *yes/no* questions.

Do you have a job?

The voice level falls within the last content word in a *wh–* question.

What kind of work do you do?

Listen and mark the intonation patterns on the following questions. Then, practise saying each sentence.

1. Is she your first girlfriend?
2. Have you seen this movie before?
3. Did they break up?
4. What kind of man are you looking for?
5. What qualities do you find attractive in a woman?
6. Are they still dating?
7. What is your idea of the perfect date?
8. Have you ever tried online dating?

Note: Different patterns of rising or falling intonation are used to add extra meaning to the question. For example, a rising intonation at the end of a *wh–* question can communicate surprise. A falling intonation on a *yes/no* question might be understood as being rude or unfriendly.

Speaking

Role play a speed-dating session with three different partners. Each speed date will last five minutes. Refer to your work in the Grammar in Use exercise on page 111 and the writing exercise on page 112 to prepare what you will say in your speed dating session.

- Make a list of fifteen useful and interesting questions you want to ask each speed date in the five minutes.

  Examples: Do you like pets?

  What is your favourite month of the year and why?

  Practise asking these questions with the appropriate intonation.

- Use the score card to indicate how well each date has performed.

	Date 1	Date 2	Date 3
This person prepared well for the date.			
This person answered all the questions I asked.			
This person asked me interesting questions.			
This person spoke clearly.			
This person made good eye contact.			
Total score			

Excellent – 3	Satisfactory – 2	Needs improvement –1

Unit Reflection

Work in same-sex teams if possible. Modern love and marriage in Canada are quite different from the traditional relationships our grandparents grew up with. Yet, in many ways they are the same. Review the chapter.

1. Compare the features of modern relationships to traditional relationships (e.g., how people meet, the dating rules, how they make decisions to marry, etc.).
2. Decide which changes you think are positive and which are negative. Why? Compare answers with other teams.

Connect all nine dots in four straight lines, without lifting your pen or pencil from the page.

What will happen to the piece of wood when the person lets go of it?

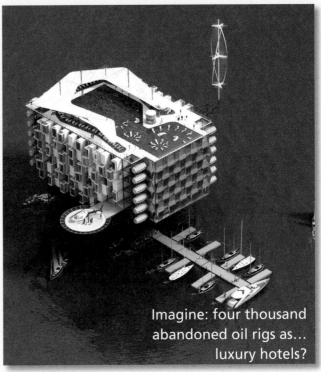

Imagine: four thousand
abandoned oil rigs as...
luxury hotels?

DISCUSSION

1. Each picture is creative in a different way. What do you think is creative about each picture?

2. Which picture do you think shows the most creativity? Why?

3. What makes something creative?

Reading

Before You Read

1. In two minutes, list as many words as you can that relate to creativity.

2. Think of the most creative person you know. Describe that person. What does the person do, think, or have that makes him or her creative? For example: That person has a lot of energy.

Imagination, Creativity, and Innovation

1 Throughout history, creative people have used their imagination to create new languages, technologies, art, stories, religions, science, math, and philosophies. Imagination is the ability to picture new ideas. It is a
5 "special sense" that allows us to go beyond the real world into a world of *possibility*—a world of ideas. Creativity is the process that makes ideas a reality. Creativity is not only expressed in art, and it is not something that only a few people are born with. All
10 humans have the potential to develop a powerful creative imagination. Imagination and creativity lead to new ways of thinking and doing things. In other words, they lead to innovation.

---

senses: smelling, hearing, seeing, touching, tasting
potential: something that can be developed in the
    future

Comprehension Check

1. What is imagination?
2. What is creativity?
3. What is innovation?

The fifteenth-century Italian artist, architect, engi-
15 neer, and scientist Leonardo da Vinci was possibly the most creative and innovative thinker of all time. Da Vinci was a great genius. He was very intelligent, but imagination and creativity were the strengths behind his innovations. In his popular book *How*
20 *to Think like Leonardo da Vinci*, Michael J. Gelb outlines seven key sources of da Vinci's creative genius.

According to Gelb, these are the principles of creativity. Understanding and developing these seven principles can help us to become more creative.

---

sources: origins
genius: someone with unusually high intelligence

Predicting

25 Creativity is like a tree. The principles (or sources) of creativity are like the roots of the tree. Without these roots, the tree cannot grow; they are the beginning of the life of the tree. They are necessary for the tree. One principle of creativity is curiosity. Before you con-
30 tinue, guess what the other six principles might be.

Develop Curiosity

The desire to know, learn, and grow leads to knowledge, wisdom, and discovery. Creativity requires a continual, strong curiosity about life. That is the first principle of creativity. Highly creative people learn
35 as much as they can about as many things as they can. They are persistent and detailed in their study of things. They are passionate about many things and they let their passion guide them to ask questions. They look at reality from extreme, unusual, and mul-
40 tiple perspectives. There are always more than two sides to any one thing. Occasionally, creative people break the rules because following tradition and being obedient interfere with creativity. Finally, creative people think about what they know and have learned.

---

continual: never-ending
persistent: keep trying and never give up
passionate: very enthusiastic, have strong positive emotions about something
perspective: point of view

Reading for Specific Information

In what lines does the following information appear?

1. Creative people are always learning new things.
2. Creative people think about what they have learned.

3. Creative people ask questions about things they are passionate about.
4. Creative people look at the real world and notice things that other people do not commonly see. They also look at things from many different perspectives.

Test Ideas in Practice

45 The second principle is that highly creative people are careful about accepting the truth of traditional wisdom. Wisdom is supposed to come from life experience. Creative people try out the wisdom passed down from generation to generation in real life. Then they
50 judge if it is true. They reject imitation, doubt existing knowledge and beliefs, and think independently. They test their ideas in practice and are willing to learn from their mistakes. Innovation is neither the result of doing things right, nor is it the result of doing
55 things wrong. Innovation comes when we learn from mistakes.

---

reject: say no to; not believe something is true
doubt: be uncertain about whether or not you should believe something

---

Comprehension Check

Creative people think independently.

1. What are three things that creative people do to show they are thinking independently?
2. What is the connection between making mistakes and innovation?

Strengthen Sensory Awareness

Sight, sound, touch, taste, and smell let you experience life fully. People feel more alive when their senses are strong. They also notice more things in their envi-
60 ronment and remember them better. Creative people deliberately improve their senses by paying close attention to them.

Reading for the Main Idea

1. Which sentence best describes the main idea of the paragraph?
    a) People feel better when they pay attention to their senses.
    b) Most people do not notice many things in the world.
    c) Creative people pay more attention to their senses.

Tolerate Uncertainty

As we mature and develop our senses and thinking processes, we realize that there are many things in
65 life we cannot know clearly. Highly creative people are patient and willing to accept uncertainty and ambiguity. Certainty is the enemy of creative thinking. Creative people deliberately look at things from contrasting perspectives.

---

ambiguity: when something is not clear

Take this self-test to see how comfortable you are with ambiguity and uncertainty. Check ✓ off each statement that describes you.

- ☐ I am comfortable with things that are unclear.
- ☐ I am aware of my intuition.
- ☐ I like change.
- ☐ I see the humour in everyday life.
- ☐ I enjoy riddles, puzzles, and jokes.
- ☐ I usually know when I am feeling uneasy or worried.
- ☐ I trust my feelings.
- ☐ I can feel comfortable when I have ideas in my mind that contradict each other.
- ☐ I like it when things contradict each other or don't make sense.
- ☐ I think that conflict is important in becoming creative.

Each statement indicates some tolerance for uncertainty and ambiguity. The more you have checked off, the more tolerant you are of uncertainty and ambiguity.

---

intuition: knowing by feeling

Reading Expansion

Look at the picture of Leonardo da Vinci's *Mona Lisa*. What is her mood? Explain how the picture supports the main idea of this paragraph.

Da Vinci's *Mona Lisa*—What is her mood?

Balance Art and Science

70 The human brain has two halves: the left hemisphere and the right hemisphere. Brain research tells us that brain activity in the left hemisphere is more involved with logical and analytical thinking. Brain activity in the right hemisphere is more involved with imagi- 75 native, intuitive, and "big picture" thinking. Artistic thinking relies more on imagination, feeling, and intu- ition, which are associated with right-brain thinking. Scientific thinking relies more on logic and systematic analysis, which are associated with left-brain thinking. 80 While all people use both hemispheres of the brain, it seems some people are right-brain dominant while others are left-brain dominant. This means that they are stronger in one style of thinking than in another. Highly creative thinkers, however, balance logical 85 thinking and imagination. Balancing artistic and sci- entific thinking is called "whole brain" thinking.

---

associated with: connected to

Reading Expansion

Write the following words under the correct heading below:

uses logic	patterns
uses feeling	fantasy
details	risk taking
rules	lists
facts	paintings
intuition	emotions
images	big picture

Left Brain	**Right Brain**

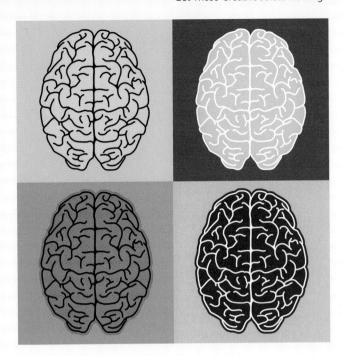

Balance Mind and Body

Balance is not just about thinking logically or intuitively. Creative people also balance the mind with the body. Physical strength and movement build energy that helps 90 thinking. At the same time, controlling the body can help to manage positive and negative emotions that result from our experiences. Therefore, it is important to be fit and develop grace.

---

grace: elegant body movements

Reading for Organization

Which outline shows the order of information given in this paragraph?

a) Balancing mind and body; building strength and elegance; controlling the body to manage emotions; increasing energy for thinking through fitness and activity

b) Balancing mind and body; increasing energy for thinking through fitness and activity; controlling the body to manage emotions; building strength and elegance

c) Balancing mind and body; controlling the body to manage emotions; building strength and elegance; increasing energy for thinking through fitness and activity

Make Connections—Systems Thinking

When a stone is tossed into a motionless pond, it
95 causes a circle of small waves that expand into wider and wider circles. One small wave affects another,

Reading to Identify Writing Technique

What technique does the writer use to end this reading?

a) The writer gives the reader an additional perspective to think about.

b) The writer uses an interesting quote to make the reader think more about the topic.

c) The writer uses controversial statements to make the reader think more about the topic.

as its energy is transferred to the next small wave. "Systems thinking" is a style of thinking that pays attention to the interconnectedness of all things and
100 experience. The expanding circle caused by a stone thrown into a pond is a good metaphor to demonstrate how things are interconnected in the world. A metaphor is a kind of comparison. Metaphors are images used to compare two things that are similar.
105 For example, we can compare life to a long trip (the journey of life) or the movement of traffic to a river (traffic flow). Metaphors help us to make connections between things.

motionless: with no movement

Reading for Meaning

In your own words, explain how the stone-in-the-pond metaphor is an example of interconnectedness.

Creativity is not an ability that only artistic people
110 are born with. With awareness and persistent practice, all people can improve their creative abilities. However, creative abilities alone are not enough. Even highly creative people need to live, learn, and work in a place that encourages and helps creativity. Some
115 environments do not encourage or support creativity. On the contrary, they may prevent human creativity. For example, new ideas will not develop in environments where everyone is expected to think and act the same way. If society wants to encourage innovation, it
120 will need both people who can think more creatively and institutions that support them.

Reading for Meaning

Each paragraph on the next page refers to one of the following topic headings. Write the corresponding number in the blank.

1. Develop Curiosity
2. Test Ideas in Practice
3. Strengthen Sensory Awareness
4. Tolerate Uncertainty
5. Balance Art and Science
6. Balance Mind and Body
7. Make Connections— Systems Thinking

a) _____ Think of the most beautiful thing you have ever seen. What is the sweetest sound you have ever heard? What has been the most wonderfully tender touch you have experienced? Imagine an exquisitely delicious taste and an intensely desirable aroma. How does each make you feel?

b) _____ In order to become more creative, direct your passion to asking questions. First, ask many questions. Some will be useful, others will not. It doesn't matter; just ask as many questions as you can. Second, ask simple questions even if the answer may be obvious. Ask challenging questions like "Who will benefit if we do it this way? Who will not?" Try to ask questions that have not been asked before. In addition, ask questions from many different perspectives. What would a child ask in this situation? What would a friend ask? What would a teacher ask?

c) _____ There are several ways to increase your health and body awareness. First, develop a fitness program that includes aerobic exercise, strength training, and flexibility exercises. Second, study your own body in the mirror. Pay attention to head balance, shoulder joints, hip joints, and your spine. Walk with straight posture. Third, do breathing exercises every day. Also, develop ambidexterity. For example, practise writing with your left hand (if you are right-handed) or with your right hand (if you are left-handed). Try drawing a simple picture with both hands at the same time.

d) _____ Begin by understanding where your personal opinions and beliefs about many topics have come from: human nature, politics, relationships, knowledge, religion, and ethics. How have your parents, teachers, religious leaders, friends, your own experience, books, the Internet, television, and newspapers influenced you in having these beliefs?

e) _____ One of the best ways to balance left- and right-brain thinking is by mind mapping. In Western thinking, people often outline ideas as a list with numeric headings such as 1, 2, 3 or A, B, C. After you have already generated your ideas, outlining is a good way to organize them; however, if you begin with an outline, you limit the range of possible ideas because you think only of ideas that fit your outline. Let's try a little thought experiment.

Think of the last movie you saw. Imagine that you have to write a movie review. Start with remembering the information and pay attention to how your mind works as you remember. Is the information presented in whole paragraphs or organized outlines? No. The impressions, key words, and images probably come into your mind in a way where one thing combines with the next.

Mind mapping works in the same way. It frees your thinking powers by allowing you to generate many different ideas and organize them at the same time.

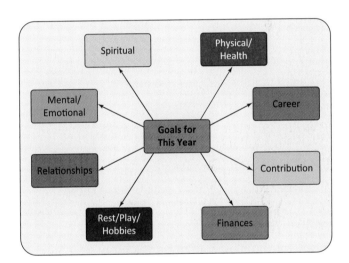

Thinking outside the Box

1. The matching exercise (Reading for Meaning) provides several suggestions for developing some of the principles of creativity. Of the seven principles, choose the one that you would most like to develop. Write an action plan to show what specific activities you will do each week to develop this creative ability. Try it for one month to see if you can make it a habit.

Example:		
To develop *curiosity*	I will *ask one question about world politics and search for the answer in the news*	*once a week.*
To develop _____	I will _____	_____ a week.

SNAPSHOT OF CANADA

Everyone knows that Canadians invented the telephone, insulin, the zipper, and basketball, but did you know that Canadian innovation also brought the world…

- Java programming (1994, James Arthur Gosling)
- BlackBerry (1999, Mike Lazaridis)
- Instant replay (1955, CBC's *Hockey Night in Canada*)
- Paint roller (1940, Norman Breakey)
- Wonderbra (1964, Louise Poirier)

Grammar Focus

Exercise A

a) Highlight the seven questions in the dialogue. Circle the signal word in each question that indicates what kind of information the question asks for.

1	Anne:	Who is the most creative person who ever lived?
2	Lenny:	I don't know. I think it was Leonardo da Vinci.
3	Anne:	Why was he the most creative?
4	Lenny:	Because he did everything. He was a painter, a designer, an inventor. He had an incredible
5		understanding of mechanics. He designed flying machines. He studied mathematics. He
6		studied plants. He was curious about so many different things.
7	Anne:	How did he become so knowledgeable?
8	Lenny:	He spent a lot of time intensely studying what interested him. He was persistent and
9		focused.
10	Anne:	When did he live?
11	Lenny:	In the late 1400s and early 1500s.
12	Anne:	Where was he from?
13	Lenny:	Don't you know where he was born?
14	Anne:	No. I thought he was French.
15	Lenny:	He died in France, but he was born and lived in Italy.
16	Anne:	What is his most famous work?
17	Lenny:	Well, he was famous for so many things, but I guess for people who don't know that
18		much about him, he is probably known as the painter of the *Mona Lisa*.

b) Contrast the *wh–* questions with the question in line number 13. What is the difference between the two types of questions?

Information Questions

In English there are two types of questions:

1. *Yes/no* questions, which can be answered with *yes* or *no. Do you speak French? Yes, I do.*

2. Information questions, whose answers provide information and cannot be answered by *yes* or *no. What is imagination? It's the ability to visualize new ideas in the mind.*

Information questions begin with an information word: *who, what, where, when, why,* and *how.*

Exercise B

1. Read the answer (A), and then write an appropriate word to make a question.
   a) A. I think it was Mozart.
      Q. _____ was the greatest musician of all time?
   b) A. It means doing something or thinking in a new way.
      Q. _____ does "innovation" mean?
   c) A. Because businesses have to come up with new ideas to stay competitive.
      Q. _____ is creative thinking important in the workplace?
   d) A. In France.
      Q. _____ did Leonardo da Vinci die?
   e) A. They always ask questions.
      Q. _____ do creative people develop their curiosity?
   f) A. Testing ideas in practice and tolerating uncertainty.
      Q. _____ are two principles of creativity?
   g) A. Mind mapping.
      Q. _____ tool can we use to balance right- and left-brain thinking?
   h) A. In the sixteenth century.
      Q. _____ did Leonardo da Vinci paint the *Mona Lisa*?

2. Look at the eight *wh–* questions above.
   - How is each question formed?
   - How are the questions alike and different from each other in their formation?

Exercise C

Write an information word on the line, and put the remaining words in the correct order to make the question. More than one word may be possible.

1. _____ can creative become people more?
2. _____ another has idea?
3. _____ is information missing?
4. _____ can improve our senses we?
5. _____ a is metaphor?
6. _____ a creative does encourage mind map thinking?
7. _____ business creativity important in is?
8. _____ creative makes something?
9. _____ did *Hamlet* Shakespeare write?
10. _____ da Vinci from was?

Exercise D

Change each statement to a question. Start the question with a *wh–* question word.

1. Research in Motion is the company that developed the BlackBerry.
2. Stanford University students Larry Page and Sergey Brin founded Google.
3. Industrial design is a mix of engineering and art.
4. A person can develop ambidexterity by writing with both hands at the same time.
5. Teachers can encourage students to take risks by not punishing them for making mistakes.
6. William Shakespeare is the best known poet of the English language.
7. Humans first landed on the moon in 1969.
8. Police should be cautious about eyewitness accounts because human memory is unreliable.
9. A person can learn about industrial design at an arts college.
10. Brainstorming is a good technique to use when you need to think of many ideas.

Exercise E

Refer to the reading on pages 116–120. Write three *what* questions, three *why* questions, and three *how* questions related to the article. Exchange your questions with a partner and write the answers to your partner's questions. Then, exchange the questions again so that you have your original questions. Check the answers for your partner.

Grammar in Use

1. Work in a group of three or four. Choose a topic that all of the group members are curious about. Brainstorm as many questions about the topic as you can in a limited time. You can include questions even if you know the answers.

2. Choose three or four interesting questions that your group doesn't know the answers to. Each group member will research and find the answer to one of those questions and report the answers back to the group.

Pronunciation Power

The end intonation pattern for *wh–* questions is different than for *yes/no* questions. Intonation in *yes/no* questions rises at the end.

Is she innovative?

Intonation in *wh–* questions rises and falls within the last content word in the sentence.

Who designed that product?

Listen to the questions in Grammar Exercise B, and mark the intonation pattern. Read the sentences aloud to practise the pattern.

Vocabulary

Word partners. What kinds of words are underlined?

1. be associated <u>with</u>
2. be aware <u>of</u>
3. be open <u>to</u>
4. be passionate <u>about</u>
5. come up <u>with</u>
6. connect (one thing) <u>to</u> (another thing)
7. focus <u>on</u>
8. improve <u>on</u>
9. lead <u>to</u>
10. pay attention <u>to</u>
11. reflect <u>on</u>
12. think <u>about</u>

Exercise A

Complete each blank with an appropriate phrase from the list above. More than one phrase may be possible.

1. A fear of making mistakes will result in taking fewer risks. A fear of making mistakes will _____ taking fewer risks.

2. Creative people accept new ideas. Creative people _____ new ideas.

3. Creative people are enthusiastic about many different things. Creative people _____ many different things.

4. Creative people notice their surroundings. Creative people _____ their surroundings.

5. How can we make this design better? How can we _____ this design?

6. If you join music with drama, you get the musical. If you _____ music _____ drama, you get the musical.

7. Let's examine what we've learned from this situation. Let's _____ what we've learned from this situation.

8. Let's concentrate on the facts of this situation. Let's _____ the facts of this situation.

9. Let's generate a list of ideas. Let's _____ a list of ideas.

10. When people think of imagination, they often think of creativity. Imagination _____ creativity.

Exercise B

On a blank page, draw nine circles. Write the words below in the circles to make nine groups of words that have similar meanings. Here is an example:

be passionate about

show enthusiasm for

have strong emotions about

accept
associate with
be aware of
connect with/to
be joined to
be open to
be passionate about
relate to

causes
come up with
create
focus on
generate
have strong emotions about
improve on
lead to

make better
pay attention to
reflect on
results in
show enthusiasm for
think about
tolerate

Vocabulary in Use

Look at the two photos with a partner and answer the following questions.

Photo A

Photo B

1. Photo A associates wires with a fork. That's unusual. What things do people normally <u>associate with</u> a fork?
2. What do you <u>focus on</u> when you look at photo B?
3. Photo A <u>connects</u> spaghetti noodles <u>to</u> wires to make something creative. What things does photo B connect?
4. In addition to sight, <u>are</u> you <u>aware of</u> any other sense when you look at photo B? What in the photo makes you <u>aware of</u> this other sense?
5. How does photo A <u>relate to</u> photo B?
6. What do you <u>pay attention to</u> when you look at photo A?

7. Based on these photos, what does a person have to <u>be open to</u> in order to create an imaginative photo?
8. How could you <u>improve on</u> photo A?
9. How could you <u>make</u> photo B <u>better</u>?
10. <u>Come up with</u> an idea for a photo that uses the same technique as these photos for stimulating the imagination.
11. Think about the message the artist is sending in these photos. What do you think the message is?
12. What <u>leads</u> you <u>to</u> say that?

Listening

Before You Listen

Look at the picture and read what the teacher says. In your mind, picture a colourful parade moving along a wide street. A youth band is marching to the beat of the music. The players are following an older band leader. One little drummer girl, however, is marching off beat. She is not in step with the other players in the band. She is marching to the beat of her own drum. The teacher is comparing his class and the young student to a parade of musicians in a marching band.

"Your daughter marches to the beat of a different drummer, but don't worry—we'll have her joining the parade by the end of term."

Discussion

1. What do you think the teacher is trying to tell the mother? What does he think of the little girl's behaviour? Why do you think the teacher wants the little girl to join the parade?
2. In the teacher's mind, what is the job of school?
3. Do you think the parade with a marching band is an accurate metaphor for what children learn in school? Why?
4. What are the advantages of learning to *march to the beat of the same drum* as others?

You will hear a story about a young girl in school. It is based on a song called "Flowers Are Red," written by a famous American singer and songwriter Harry Chapin. In the original song, the young student was a boy. The story is true. It happened to the eleven-year-old son of Chapin's secretary. In this story, the young child is a girl.

Listening for the Main Idea

In your words, tell the main idea of the story. What is the lesson of the story?

Listening for Specific Information

The teachers and the little girl had very different ideas about (1) what to make and (2) how to make it. Listen to Excerpts 1, 2, and 3 again and write key words on the easels to describe these differences.

Excerpt 1

Excerpt 2

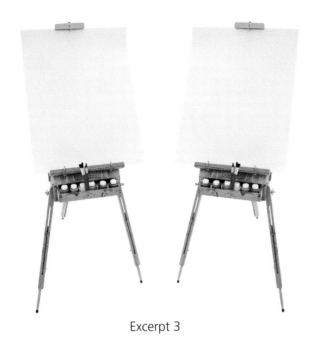

Excerpt 3

Listening to Retell a Story

Listen again. Write down key words to help you remember the details of the story. Share your details with two other classmates. Together, rewrite the story using as many details from the original story as you can. Compare your story to the original by listening again.

Thinking outside the Box

Offer a different interpretation of the cartoon at the beginning of the Listening section.

Writing

Think back to your early years in school. How did the school system and your classroom teachers encourage or discourage your creativity? Remember one story as an example. Write down some key words to help you tell the story to a partner. Your partner will ask you five to six questions to get more details. Use your notes and your partner's questions to write the story.

Speaking

Problem solving—developing creativity in schools

Some people think our education system could do a better job to help students develop their creative potential. Think about your own school experiences. How do schools encourage creativity and how do they discourage it? You are a member of a student advisory group, which will give advice to leaders in education. Use the Six-Thinking-Hats technique on this page to make three recommendations for what schools can do to develop students' creative potential. Your teacher will tell you how much time to spend with each coloured hat and may ask you to present your recommendations to the class.

The Six Thinking Hats

This is a technique developed by Dr. Edward de Bono for group problem solving. The idea of wearing a hat is a metaphor. The group should only "wear one hat at a time" when considering a problem. In other words, it should look at the problem from only one perspective, the perspective indicated by the hat colour. One person will wear the blue hat and decide which order the group will follow for wearing a coloured hat.

 **Blue hat**—Consider the "big picture." Give this hat to only one person in the group. That person will control the thinking process of the group by deciding which order the group will follow for wearing the other hats.

 **Black hat**—Be critical. Criticize all ideas and consider what cannot be done.

 **Yellow hat**—Be positive. Discuss <u>only</u> the positive views of the problem. Look for benefits.

 **White hat**—Remain neutral. Consider the data and information you have and need to make a good decision.

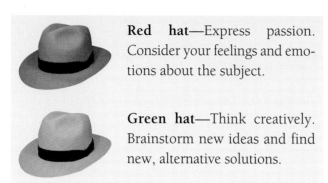

Red hat—Express passion. Consider your feelings and emotions about the subject.

Green hat—Think creatively. Brainstorm new ideas and find new, alternative solutions.

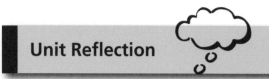

Unit Reflection

Work in small groups. Use the Six-Thinking-Hats technique to reflect on this unit. On a large piece of paper, copy the Six-Thinking-Hats mind map below.

Each discussion point below matches one hat colour. Decide which coloured hat matches each discussion point. As you discuss the point, write key words on the branches of the matching hat to show your ideas. Be prepared to explain your map. Assign one person to wear the blue hat and be the group manager.

Discuss

- the information and facts presented in the unit and what you can learn from them
- your feelings and emotions about the information in this unit
- the concerns and problems you have with the information in this unit. What might not work?
- the positive aspects and benefits of the information in the unit
- creative solutions to encourage creativity in learners and workers

Unit 10
That's So Canadian

DISCUSSION

1. This image is an internationally recognized symbol for Canada. What does it represent?

2. What are some internationally recognized symbols for your home country? How accurately do these symbols reflect life in your country?

3. What role do national symbols play in people's perception of a country?

Listening

Before You Listen

Discuss which images refer to Canadian cultural and which refer to other cultures.

Listening for the Gist

Listen to the entire passage and answer the questions.

1. In what context does this conversation happen?
2. What is the relationship between the speakers? How do you know?
3. What is the tone of this conversation?
4. What is the talk about?
5. Which of the images in the Before You Listen exercise are discussed in the excerpt? Check the boxes of the photos.

Listening for Key Words

Write one sentence for each excerpt that identifies a common image people have of Canadians.

> *Example:*
> Excerpt 1—Canadians are friendly.

Thinking outside the Box

Add one excerpt to the listening passage by writing a short dialogue that explains an additional common image people have of Canadians.

Speaking

It is acceptable to say "no" to an invitation or a request, but we are expected to do so politely. There are many ways to politely say "no." As a rule, begin your response with a positive phrase or apology and then give a reason.

> *I'm sorry, (but) . . .*
> *I'd really like to, but . . .*
> *I wish I could, but . . .*
> *I'm afraid I can't.*
> *I would (if I could), but . . .*

Rejecting an invitation

When rejecting an invitation, the reason you give may be general or specific.

I: Would you like to come for a barbecue at my place on Sunday?
I'm sorry, (but) I'm busy. (general)
I'm sorry, (but) I'm going to a baseball game on Sunday. (specific)

I: Why don't you come camping with us next weekend?
I'd really like to, but I have other plans.
I'd really like to, but I'm going to a friend's cottage next weekend.

I: Do you want to see a hockey game this weekend?
I wish I could, but I can't.
I wish I could, but I have a test next week and I have to study.

Refusing a request

When refusing a request, it is more polite to give a specific reason.

R: Do you think you could lend me some money? I forgot my wallet.
I'm sorry, (but) I don't have any cash on me.

R: Could you give me a ride to the airport tomorrow?
I'm afraid I can't. I'm having a problem with my car. It's in the shop.

R: Would you mind picking up a book for me when you go to the library this afternoon?
I would, but I'm going before it opens. I'm just going to drop my book in the drop box outside.

Exercise A

Work with a partner to practise short dialogues. Use the prompts below to make an invitation or request and politely reject or refuse it. You will need to decide on the context.

1. borrow a stranger's newspaper

2. make a dentist appointment immediately

3. get change for a twenty-dollar bill

4. get a classmate's phone number

5. borrow a classmate's electronic dictionary

6. pay by cheque

7. leave class early

8. borrow a classmate's notes

9. take a photo of a stranger's baby

10. attend a hockey game with you

11. study at a library with a friend

12. celebrate a cultural holiday

Vocabulary

Exercise A

Complete the crossword puzzle below with the words from the list. Leave a space between answers that are two words.

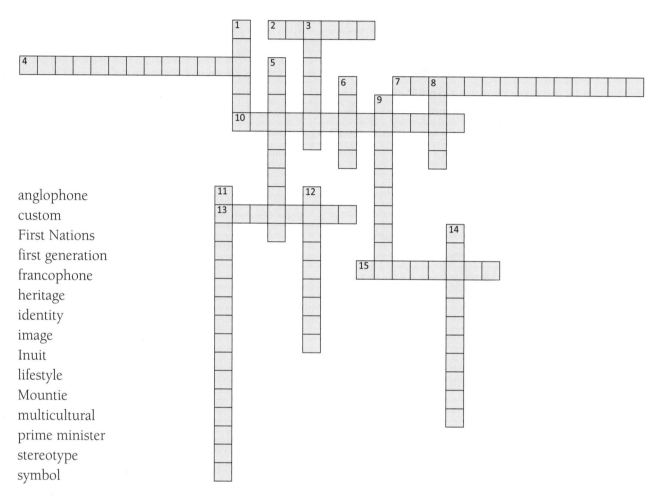

anglophone
custom
First Nations
first generation
francophone
heritage
identity
image
Inuit
lifestyle
Mountie
multicultural
prime minister
stereotype
symbol

Across

2. image or object that represents something else
4. one of the groups of people who were the first to live in Canada
7. the leader of Canada
10. made up of different cultures
13. the qualities of a person or group that define them as different from others
15. the shared history and culture that describes a group

Down

1. a usual behaviour in a society or community
3. an officer of the Royal Canadian Mounted Police
5. a person who speaks English as his or her main language
6. the Aboriginal peoples from northern Canada and Greenland
8. a mental picture
9. an idea or belief that people have of someone belonging to a particular group, but which is over-generalized or is often not true
11. the first group of people in a family to be born in Canada
12. the way people live and work
14. a person who speaks French as their main language

Exercise B

Circle the word that fits the blank.

1. Canadians feel a strong connection to the land and the cold climate. Both are important to the Canadian _____.
   identity / stereotype / symbols
2. Canadian-born children whose grandparents immigrated to Canada are considered _____ Canadians.
   first-generation / second-generation / third-generation
3. The people of northern Canada are called the _____. francophones / Inuit / First Nations
4. Barbecuing outdoors at the first sign of warm weather is a great Canadian _____.
   image / identity / custom
5. Canada has the highest per capita immigration rate in the world. That's one reason cities like Vancouver and Toronto are so _____.
   symbolic / anglophone / multicultural
6. Canadians generally love the outdoors. Hiking, biking, barbecuing, canoeing, and camping are part of the Canadian _____.
   heritage / lifestyle / symbols
7. The maple leaf is more than a leaf on a tree. It is a(n) _____ of Canada's wilderness.
   image / symbol / stereotype
8. The belief that Canadians generally dislike the US is a _____. that may not be true.
   custom / heritage / stereotype
9. People around the world have a(n) _____. of Canadians as friendly and polite.
   identity / lifestyle / image
10. The most popular image of a(n) _____ is that of a proud officer in a red coat and brown hat, riding a horse and carrying a Canadian flag.
    Mountie / Inuit / prime minister
11. Most Canadians are _____. Their main language is English.
    anglophones / First Nations / francophones
12. A distinct French influence is an important part of Canada's _____.
    heritage / stereotype / multiculturalism
13. More than 85 percent of Canadians who speak French as their main language live in Quebec. Half the _____ who live outside Quebec live in Ontario and a quarter live in New Brunswick.
    anglophones / First Nations / francophones
14. The leader of the government of Canada is the _____.
    Mountie / prime minister / francophone
15. One of the groups of the original people of Canada is called (the) _____ people.
    First Nations / Inuit / multicultural

Vocabulary in Use

Create a collage for your home culture. Include visuals that give information about the following:

identity	multiculturalism	image
symbols	lifestyle	heritage
customs	stereotypes	

Be prepared to use the vocabulary words to explain your collage to other classmates

Grammar Focus

Exercise A

I arrived in Canada on a **cold February morning**₁ thirty years ago. An **ice-cold wind**₂ blew across the **airport tarmac**₃ in Toronto as we exited the **airplane**₄. The **coat**₅ I was wearing could not keep out the **cold wind**₆. There was only one terminal in those days. When we entered the **building**₇ a **kind man**₈ in a **uniform**₉ greeted us with a **big smile**₁₀. "Welcome to Canada," he said.

1. Circle the word before each word or phrase in bold.
2. What information do the words *a/an* or *the* give us about the word or phrase that follows?
3. How are *a/an* and *the* used differently? Describe the pattern you see.

One way to give more information about a noun is to use an article (the, a/an). Articles tell us whether or not the noun is specific and identifiable in the situation. *The* indicates that the noun is specific and identifiable. *A/an* indicates that the noun is not specific or identifiable.

- Articles always come before the noun, never after (e.g., a tourist).
- Articles are always in the first position of a noun phrase (e.g., the curious tourist).
- When using *a/an*, use *an* if the word that follows begins with a vowel sound and *a* if the word that follows begins with a consonant sound.

Deciding Which Article to Use

Before you can make a decision about which article to use, you must know two things about the noun.

1. Is the noun countable (e.g., airplane) or uncountable (e.g., wind)?

2. Is the noun unspecified (indefinite) or specified (definite)?

Unspecified (Indefinite) Noun

With an unspecified noun, the reader or listener does not know exactly which *one* or *ones* you mean by the noun.

Example: I met a tourist on the bus. (Which tourist? The reader or listener does not know the specific tourist. It could be any tourist on the bus.)

Specified (Definite) Noun

With a specified noun, the reader or listener can imagine or assume exactly which noun you are talking about.

Example: The tourist I met on the bus yesterday was from India. (Which tourist? The reader or listener knows that it is the tourist you met yesterday on the bus who is from India.)

Exercise B

Complete the text with *a*, *an*, or *the* where they are necessary. If no word is necessary, write Ø. Listen to the passage to hear the answers.

I remember my first day at work in 1 _____ **Canada**. It was 2 _____ **small company**. My boss welcomed me and introduced me to 3 _____ **other employees** in 4 _____ **office**. Everyone was very friendly and helpful. 5 _____ **woman** who sat beside me invited me to lunch. We both ate 6 _____ **big salad** and drank 7 _____ **coffee**. 8 _____ **salad** was very good. I was happy that 9 _____ **Jennifer** had invited me to lunch. She was 10 _____ **very kind person**. In 11 _____ **last two** years I have developed 12 _____ **good friendships** with several of my co-workers.

There are many rules for using articles. They can be difficult to use correctly. This flow chart can help you to decide whether to use *a/an*, *the*, or no article (Ø).

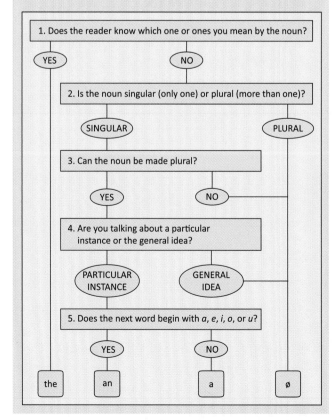

1. Does the reader know which one or ones you mean by the noun?
   - YES
   - NO
2. Is the noun singular (only one) or plural (more than one)?
   - SINGULAR
   - PLURAL
3. Can the noun be made plural?
   - YES
   - NO
4. Are you talking about a particular instance or the general idea?
   - PARTICULAR INSTANCE
   - GENERAL IDEA
5. Does the next word begin with *a, e, i, o,* or *u*?
   - YES
   - NO

the | an | a | ø

General Idea / Particular Instance

Are you talking about a particular instance or a general idea?

Some nouns can be used both as countable and uncountable nouns. Abstract nouns frequently fall under this category (e.g., freedom, experience). Concrete nouns such as *school* and *rock* can also be used this way.

- When you use these nouns as countable nouns (as a plural, or as a singular form with *a/an*), you are telling the reader or listener to think about the noun as a particular instance.

- When you use these nouns as uncountable nouns (a singular noun with no article), you tell the reader or listener to think of the noun as a general idea.

Example:

Particular instance: Canadian children generally attend *a school* in their neighbourhood.

The writer or speaker wants us to think about a particular school in the neighbourhood.

General idea: Canadian children often begin *school* at age four.

The writer or speaker wants us to think of school as a general idea.

Exercise C

Use the flow chart on page 134 to help you complete the text with *a/an, the,* or no article (Ø). Then, check that your answers have not broken any of the rules for using articles on page 158 in the Appendix.

a) 1 _____ **maple leaf** is 2 _____ **important symbol** of 3 _____ **Canada**.

b) 1 _____ **Canadian flag** has 2 _____ **red maple leaf**.

c) 1 _____ **Hockey** is 2 _____ **national sport** of 3 _____ **Canada**.

d) Most Canadian children learn to play 1 _____ **hockey**.

e) 1 _____ **Royal Canadian Mounted Police** is 2 _____ **national police force** of 3 _____ **Canada**.

f) 1 _____ **Canada** has 2 _____ **prime minister**, not 3 _____ **president**.

g) 1 _____ **Maurice Richard** was 2 _____ **famous Canadian hockey player**.

h) 1 _____ **French** and 2 _____ **English** are 3 _____ **two official languages of Canada**.

i) 1 _____ **main job** of 2 _____ **Canadian army** around 3 _____ **world** is 4 _____ **peacekeeping**.

j) 1 _____ **weather** in 2 _____ **Canada** plays 3 _____ **important role** in 4 _____ **people's lives**.

Pronunciation Power

The pronunciation of *a* /ə/ and *the* /ðə/ is the same except for the initial /ð/ sound of *the*.

Exercise A

Listen and circle the article you hear. Then, listen again and repeat each phrase.

1. *a/the* cold wind
2. *a/the* newcomer to Canada
3. *a/the* hockey sweater
4. *a/the* baseball game
5. *a/the* beaver
6. *a/the* Mountie
7. *a/the* backpack
8. *a/the* custom

Exercise B

Listen and circle the article you hear. Then, listen again and repeat each sentence.

1. Paul emailed me *a/the* photo of Niagara Falls.
2. Victor keeps Canadian Tire money in *a/the* kitchen drawer.
3. He wants *a/the* maple-sugar doughnut.

4. She sewed *a/the* Canadian flag on her backpack.
5. We're going fishing in *a/the* rowboat.
6. Are you going to *a/the* hockey game?
7. Officer Dale rode *a/the* horse.
8. She lives in *a/the* city.

- When *the* precedes a noun that begins with a vowel sound, its pronunciation changes from /ðə/ to /ðɪ/

Listen to and repeat the pronunciation of *the* in the phrases.

the artist	the Canadian artist
the image	the most popular image
the identity	the person's identity
the Inuit	the Canadian Inuit
the election	the provincial election

Exercise C

Take turns reading the sentences to a partner using *a* or *the*. Your partner will circle the article he or she hears.

1. *A/The* Canadian team won.
2. We saw *a/the* moose on the road.
3. Vince dialed *a/the* wrong number.
4. I'll be there within *a/the* week.
5. Linda bought *a/the* car last month.
6. I'm trying to listen to *a/the* weather forecast.
7. *A/The* warm wind blew across the Prairies.
8. *A/The* Canadian athlete won *a/the* medal.
9. *A/The* politician wrote *a/the* book.
10. *A/The* Canadian invented this.

Exercise D

Work with a partner to complete the following passage with an appropriate article or no article. Discuss the reasons for your choices.

1 _____ Canadian parents believe that their job is to prepare their children to live independently. 2 _____ Canadian parents would consider themselves unsuccessful if their adult children still lived at home after they had finished their education. 3 _____ Canadian children want to grow up to be different than their parents and have 4 _____ life of their own. 5 _____ Public schools don't have 6 _____ uniforms.

7 _____ Students are encouraged to express and develop their unique talents in 8 _____ after-school activities and 9 _____ clubs. Many older people fear that they will become dependent on their children later in 10 _____ life.

Grammar in Use

Write a paragraph like the one in Exercise D. Explain what your home culture thinks about raising children. Use the flow chart to help you decide which articles to use. Check that you have not broken any of the rules about using articles on page 158 in the Appendix.

Reading

Before You Read

1. List three or four stereotypes that exist about people from your home country,
2. There is more to a country and its people than its stereotypes. What do you want the world to know about the citizens of your country? Write two statements to show that the people in your country are more than a stereotype.

Poetry

A poetry slam is a competition where poets recite or read a poem they have written. Poetry slams are very political. The poems talk about important social, economic, and political issues. Poets are judged not only on the content of their poems, but also on the passion of their speech. At the 2010 Winter Olympics in Vancouver, slam poet Shayne Koyczan recited the poem "We Are More" before millions of people. Listen to your teacher read the poem as you read along for the first time. Then read it again on your own.

"We Are More"

by Shane Koyczan

When defining Canada
you might list some statistics
you might mention our tallest building
or biggest lake
5 you might shake a tree in the fall
and call a red leaf Canada
you might rattle off some celebrities
might mention Buffy Sainte-Marie
might even mention the fact that we've got a few
10 Barenaked Ladies
or that we made these crazy things
like zippers
electric cars
and washing machines

15 When defining Canada
it seems the world's anthem has been
"been there done that"
and maybe that's where we used to be at
it's true
20 we've done and we've been
we've seen
all the great themes get swallowed up by the machine
and turned into theme parks

But when defining Canada
25 don't forget to mention that we have set sparks
we are not just fishing stories
about the one that got away
we do more than sit around and say "eh?"
and yes
30 we are the home of the Rocket and the Great One
who inspired little number nines
and little number ninety-nines
but we're more than just hockey and fishing lines
off of the rocky coast of the Maritimes
35 and some say what defines us
is something as simple as please and thank you
and as for you're welcome
well we say that too

but we are more
40 than genteel or civilized
we are an idea in the process
of being realized
we are young
we are cultures strung together
45 then woven into a tapestry
and the design
is what makes us more
than the sum total of our history
we are an experiment going right for a change
50 with influences that range from a to zed
and yes we say zed instead of zee
we are the colours of Chinatown and the coffee of Little Italy
we dream so big that there are those
55 who would call our ambition an industry
because we are more than sticky maple syrup and clean snow
we do more than grow wheat and brew beer
we are vineyards of good year after good year
60 we reforest what we clear
because we believe in generations beyond our own
knowing now that so many of us
have grown past what used to be
we can stand here today
65 filled with all the hope people have
when they say things like "someday"
someday we'll be great
someday we'll be this
or that
70 someday we'll be at a point
when someday was yesterday
and all of our aspirations will pay the way
for those who on that day
look towards tomorrow
75 and still they say someday
we will reach the goals we set
and we will get interest on our inspiration
because we are more than a nation of whale watch-
ers and lumberjacks
80 more than backpacks and hiking trails
we are hammers and nails building bridges
towards those who are willing to walk across
we are the lost-and-found for all those who might
find themselves at a loss

85 we are not the see-through gloss or glamour
of those who clamour for the failings of others
we are fathers brothers sisters and mothers
uncles and nephews aunts and nieces
we are cousins
90 we are found missing puzzle pieces
we are families with room at the table for newcomers
we are more than summers and winters
more than on and off seasons
we are the reasons people have for wanting to stay
95 because we are more than what we say or do
we live to get past what we go through
and learn who we are
we are students
students who study the studiousness of studying
100 so we know what as well as why
we don't have all the answers
but we try
and the effort is what makes us more
we don't all know what it is in life we're looking for
105 so keep exploring
go far and wide
or go inside but go deep
go deep
as if James Cameron was filming a sequel to *The Abyss*
110 and suddenly there was this location scout
trying to figure some way out
to get inside you
because you've been through hell and high water
and you went deep
115 keep exploring
because we are more
than a laundry list of things to do and places to see
we are more than hills to ski
or countryside ponds to skate
120 we are the abandoned hesitation of all those who
can't wait
we are first-rate greasy-spoon diners and healthy-
living cafes
a country that is all the ways you choose to live
125 a land that can give you variety
because we are choices
we are millions upon millions of voices shouting
"keep exploring . . . we are more"
we are the surprise the world has in store for you
130 it's true

Canada is the "what" in "what's new?"
so don't say "been there done that"
unless you've sat on the sidewalk
while chalk artists draw still lifes
135 on the concrete of a kid in the street
beatboxing to Neil Young for fun
don't say you've been there done that
unless you've been here doing it
let this country be your first-aid kit
140 for all the times you get sick of the same old same old
let us be the story told to your friends
and when that story ends
leave chapters for the next time you'll come back
next time pack for all the things
145 you didn't pack for the first time
but don't let your luggage define your travels
each life unravels differently
and experiences are what make up
the colours of our tapestry
150 we are the true north
strong and free
and what's more
is that we didn't just say it
we made it be.

Reading for the Main Idea

Choose the sentence that states the main idea.

a) ☐ Canada is more than the sum of its parts.
b) ☐ Canada is more beautiful than any other place in the world.
c) ☐ Canada will be more important to the world in the future than it is today.
d) ☐ Canada is more than the popular images people have about it.

Reading for Specific Information

The poet states that Canada is *more than* the images people commonly have about it.

1. In the first section of the poem, the poet describes some of the common images people have about Canada by talking about how people *define* Canada (*when defining Canada . . .*). Read through the first section of the poem. In the first maple leaf, write a list of five or six images that commonly define Canada.

2. In the long passage in the middle of the poem, Koyczan signals other common images of Canada with the phrases *we are not just . . .*, *we are more than . . .*, and *we do more than . . .* these things. Read this section of the poem to identify at least ten other images that commonly define Canada. Write them in the second maple leaf.

Reading for Meaning

1. The poet does not deny the relevance of these common images, but he wants people to know that Canada is more than this. Read the following two passages from the poem and explain what the poet is trying to say in each:
   a) Passage: lines 44–51
   b) Passage: lines 122–130

2. Read the following lines from the poem and explain the meaning:
   a) we are an idea in the process of being realized (lines 41–42)
   b) and yes we say zed instead of zee (line 51)
   c) we are the lost-and-found for all those who might find themselves at a loss (lines 83–84)
   d) we are found missing puzzle pieces (line 90)
   e) we are families with room at the table for newcomers (line 91)
   f) we are the true north strong and free and what's more is that we didn't just say it we made it be. (lines 150–154)

Thinking outside the Box

Write a cinquain poem about your life in Canada. A cinquain poem expresses brief thoughts. It has five lines and follows this pattern:

1. NOUN
2. ADJECTIVE, ADJECTIVE (description)
3. VERBing, VERBing, VERBing (gerund)
4. PHRASE (feeling)
5. NOUN (synonym of the original noun)

Example:

Canada
peaceful, free
laughing, growing, changing,
tolerant of difference
hope

Writing

With a partner, write lyrics describing Canada to the tune of "Jingle Bells."

Unit Reflection

Work in small groups. Redesign the Canadian flag based on what you have learned in this unit. Be prepared to explain your design to classmates.

Grammar Reference

Verb Chart

V₁	V_ing	V₂	V₃
become	becoming	became	become
begin	beginning	began	begun
bleed	bleeding	bled	bled
break	breaking	broke	broken
bring	bringing	brought	brought
build	building	built	built
burn	burning	burnt/burned	burnt/burned
buy	buying	bought	bought
catch	catching	caught	caught
choose	choosing	chose	chosen
come	coming	came	come
cost	costing	cost	cost
cut	cutting	cut	cut
dig	digging	dug	dug
draw	drawing	drew	drawn
drink	drinking	drank	drunk
drive	driving	drove	driven
eat	eating	ate	eaten
fall	falling	fell	fallen
feed	feeding	fed	fed
feel	feeling	felt	felt
fight	fighting	fought	fought
find	finding	found	found
fit	fitting	fit	fit
flee	fleeing	fled	fled
fly	flying	flew	flown
forget	forgetting	forgot	forgotten
forgive	forgiving	forgave	forgiven
get	getting	got	gotten
give	giving	gave	given
go	going	went	gone
grow	growing	grew	grown

V₁	Vₑₙ₉	V₂	V₃
hide	hiding	hid	hidden
hit	hitting	hit	hit
hear	hearing	heard	heard
hold	holding	held	held
hurt	hurting	hurt	hurt
keep	keeping	kept	kept
know	knowing	knew	known
lead	leading	led	led
leave	leaving	left	left
lend	lending	lent	lent
lie (recline)	lying	lay	lain
lose	losing	lost	lost
mean	meaning	meant	meant
meet	meeting	met	met
pay	paying	paid	Paid
put	putting	put	Put
read	reading	read	read
ride	riding	rode	Ridden
rise	rising	rose	risen
see	seeing	saw	seen
show	showing	showed	showed/shown
shoot	shooting	shot	shot
sing	singing	sang	sung
sit	sitting	sat	sat
smell	smelling	smelt	smelt
speak	speaking	spoke	spoken
spend	spending	spent	spent
stand	standing	stood	stood
steal	stealing	stole	stolen
swim	swimming	swam	swum
take	taking	took	taken
teach	teaching	taught	taught
throw	throwing	threw	thrown
think	thinking	thought	thought
understand	understanding	understood	understood
wear	wearing	wore	worn
write	writing	wrote	written

Chapter 4

Pronunciation Power, Exercise D

Partner B should read either sentence a or b of each pair to Partner A.

1. a) Six or seven percent of teen social networkers say they update their Facebook page at least once a week.

   b) Sixty-seven percent of teen social networkers say they update their Facebook page at least once a week.

2. a) In the US, one-half of online users twelve to seventy visited MySpace and Facebook in May.

   b) In the US, nearly half of online users twelve to seventeen visited MySpace and Facebook in May.

3. a) Fifty-seven percent of teen social networkers said they looked to their online social network for advice.

   b) Five to seven percent of teen social networkers said they looked to their online social network for advice.

4. a) More than two-thirds of teens download ringtones, Instant Message, or use the mobile Web, while about three-quarters download music.

   b) More than a third of teens download ringtones, Instant Message, or use the mobile Web, while about a quarter download music.

5. a) Forty-five percent of teens globally say they listen to five or more hours of music per week on their computer.

   b) Forty-five percent of teens globally say they listen to three or four hours of music per week on their computer.

Unit 1: Hero to the Rescue!

Adverbs of Manner

An adverb is a word that is used to describe or modify a verb, an adjective, another adverb, a clause, or a sentence. An adverb of manner describes *how* something is done.

Placement of Adverbs of Manner

1. The adverb of manner can be placed at the beginning of the sentence to get our attention.

   Examples:

   Carefully, the firefighter entered the burning building.

   Persistently, he fought for the rights of children.

In these sentences, *carefully* and *persistently* are emphasized. They modify the entire clause.

2. Adverbs of a manner can also be found in the middle of a sentence. This is common in sentences that do not have an adverb of frequency.

   Examples:

   He **strongly** encouraged peaceful protest.
   They have **consistently** fought racism.

In the first sentence, the adverb of manner comes before the verb. In the second sentence, the adverb comes between the auxiliary and the verb. In these sentences, the adverbs modify the verbs.

3. If there is an object in the sentence, the adverb often comes after the object. However, if there is a preposition before the object, the adverb can be placed either before the preposition or after the object.

   Examples:

   Nelson Mandela received the Nobel Prize **graciously**.

   Mahatma Ghandi protested **peacefully** against injustice.

   Mahatma Ghandi protested against injustice **peacefully**.

4. If the adverb of manner is used to describe an adjective or another adverb, it usually goes before the word it is describing.

   Example:

   She is **extremely** happy with the results.

You will hear adverbs of manner used in the following way, often to make the sentence more forceful:

Examples:

To **boldly** go where no man has gone before.

They decided to **loudly** protest against human rights abuses.

Inserting an adverb of manner between *to* and the base form of the verb has become common in recent years. However, both of these sentences are considered incorrect in formal English because they split the infinitive. Following formal grammatical rules, these sentences would be:

Examples:

To go **boldly** where no man has gone before.

They decided to protest **loudly** against human rights abuses.

Spelling Adverbs That End in –ly

We can form many adverbs by adding –ly to an adjective or verb.

Examples:

terrible—terribly
consistent—consistently
willing—willingly
determined—determinedly

Adjectives ending in –l or –e: add ly

wonderfu**l** + ly = wonderfully
nic**e** + ly = nicely

*there are a few exceptions to this rule

Adjectives ending in –ic: add –ally

tragic + ally = tragically
heroic + ally = heroically
exception: public – publicly

Adjectives ending in –able or –ible: drop the e and add y

terrib**le** + y = terribly
capab**le** + y = capably

Adjectives ending in a consonant + –le: drop the e and add y

no**ble** + y = nobly
gen**tle** + y = gently

Adjectives ending in –y: drop the y and add –ily

bus**y** + ily = busily
happ**y** + ily = happily

Unit 2: Ancient Secrets Revealed

Past Time Tense Considerations

There are two points to consider when deciding which tense to use:

1. the time when an action occurs

We help the listener or reader understand our time perspective by using verb tenses (verb forms that show time). We can also use time expressions, such as *yesterday, last month, by 1950, in the 18th century,* and *two hundred years ago.* Usually we combine verb tenses and time expressions.

2. the relationship of the action to the time

We can think of actions as having four possible relationships to time. An action can be:

at that time;
in progress *during* that time;
before that time; or
in progress *during* and *before* that time

Tense	Use	Example
Simple Past	1. activity that began and finished at a specific time in the past	They discovered the crop circles last night.
	2. actions, states, or situations that are finished	He was the first Emperor of China.

Now

Past ———×——┼—Future→

Artisans created the Terracotta warriors.

S + V$_2$: *They found the pottery warriors in a field.*

S + did + not + V$_1$: *They didn't find the pottery warriors in a field.*

Did + S + V$_1$? *Did they find the pottery warriors in a field?*

Did + not + S + V$_1$? *Didn't they find the pottery warriors in a field?*

Wh– word + did + S + V$_1$? *Where did they find the pottery warriors?*

Tense	Use	Example
Past Progressive/ Continuous	1. past activity that was in progress when it was interrupted by another action in the past	They were eating breakfast when the volcano erupted.
	2. past activity that was in progress (used to describe a background scene)	It was a normal morning. The family was eating breakfast.
	3. past activity that was in progress for a time	They were building the temple.
	4. past activities that were in progress during the same period	Some workers were digging while others were carrying stones.

Now

enemy attacked

Past ———×——┼—Future→

preparing for war

They were preparing for war when the enemy attacked.

S + was/were + Ving: *They were planning to visit.*

S + was/were + not + Ving: *They were not planning to visit.*

Was/were + S + Ving? *Were they planning to visit?*

Was/were + S + not + Ving? *Were they not planning to visit?*

Was/were + not + S + Ving? *Weren't they planning to visit?*

Wh– word + was/were + S + Ving? *When were they planning to visit?*

Tense	Use	Example
Past Perfect	past activity that was completed before another event/time	Thieves had already stolen many items before the archeologists excavated the tomb.

Now

had finished   emperor died

Past ——— $\times_1$ ——— $\times_2$ ——|—— Future ➤

They had finished$_1$ when the emperor died$_2$.

S + had (not) + V$_3$ when + S +V$_2$: *The artisans hadn't finished their work when the emperor died.*

Had + S + V$_3$ when S + V$_2$? *Had the artisans finished their work when the emperor died?*

Tense	Use	Example
Past Perfect Progressive	emphasis on how long a past activity was in progress before and up to another past event/time	People had been searching for the treasure for years when it was discovered.

Past Perfect Progressive/ Continuous

Now

emperor died

building tomb

Past ——— 1 $\times_2$ ——|—— Future ➤

They had been building$_1$ the tomb when the emperor died$_2$.

S + had + been + Ving when + S +V$_2$: *They had been digging for a long time when they discovered the clay head.*

S + had (not) + been + Ving when + S +V$_2$: *They hadn't been digging for a long time when they discovered the clay head.*

Had + S + been + Ving when S + V$_2$? *Had they been digging for a long time when they discovered the clay head?*

Had + S + not + been + Ving when S + V$_2$? *Had they not been digging for a long time when they discovered the clay head?*

Had + not + S + been + Ving when S + V$_2$? *Hadn't they been digging for a long time when they discovered the clay head?*

Wh– word + had + S + been + Ving when S + V$_2$? *Where had they been digging when they discovered the clay head?*

Forming the Simple Past

The simple past of regular verbs is formed by adding –*d* or –*ed* to the base form of the verb.

- If the verb ends in a consonant, add –*ed* (e.g., construct ⟶ constructed).
- If the verb ends in *e*, add –*d* (e.g., excavate ⟶ excavated).
- If the verb ends in a consonant + *y*, change the *y* to *i*, and add –*ed* (e.g., bury ⟶ buried).
- If the verb ends in a vowel + *y*, add –*ed* (e.g., play ⟶ played).
- If the verb is one syllable and the last three letters are consonant, vowel, consonant (CVC), double the final consonant (except: *w*, *x*, or *y*) and add –*ed* (e.g., stop ⟶ stopped). This rule also applies for verbs of two or more syllables when the last syllable is stressed (e.g., permit ⟶ permitted).

Unit 3: O Canada, Je t'aime

Quantifiers

Quantifiers (determiners) are words or phrases that indicate the quantity or number of something.

Singular Countable Nouns	Plural Countable Nouns	Uncountable Nouns
any (one of a number of things; not important which one) *Any region that has its own government is a province or territory.*	**any** (one of a number of things; not important which one) *I'll buy any paintings by a Group of Seven artist.*	**little** (a small amount of something) *The railroad workers earned little money.*
each (refers to a fact that is common to all members of a group, but emphasizes the individual member) *Each province has its own capital city.*	**both** (refers to two people or things together) *Both central provinces border Hudson Bay.*	**much** (a large amount; to a large degree) *Canada has much fresh water.*
every (refers to a single member of a group, but emphasizes a fact that is common to all members) *Every province has a capital city.*	**few** (not enough; limited) *Few people in Nunavut are Francophones.*	**all** (every; the entire amount) *All water in the Great Lakes is fresh.*
numerals (a particular quantity) *One province is on the west coast.*	**many** (a large number of) *Many provinces border oceans.*	**most** (almost all) *Most fresh water in Canada comes from the Great Lakes.*
either (a choice between two) *Either Nunavut or Yukon has the smallest population.*	**several** (some; smaller than many) *Several provinces have mountains.*	**some** (an amount that is unknown or not stated) *It is easier to understand Canadian culture if you know some Canadian history.*
neither (not either of two things or people) *Neither central province is on the coast.*	**half** (either of two equal or nearly equal parts) *Half the provinces border oceans.*	
	all (the total number of) *All provinces have a capital city.*	
	most (the biggest number or amount of) *Most people live close to the US border.*	
	some (an amount that is unknown or not stated) *Some people live in isolated areas.*	

Placement of Quantifiers

Quantifiers are determiners that come before the adjective and noun in a noun phrase.

Agreement with the Quantifier

When the quantifier precedes a noun or noun phrase in the subject position, the verb agrees in number with the quantifier. Some quantifiers are singular, some are plural, and some may be either.

- Quantifiers that modify a singular countable noun take the 1st person verb form.
- Quantifiers that modify a plural countable noun take the 3rd person verb form.
- Quantifiers that modify an uncountable noun take the 3rd person verb form.
- Quantifiers that modify a collective noun take either a singular or plural verb form, depending on whether you want to emphasize the single group or its individual members.

Quantifier + of

- If you want to quantify a noun that is specific and identifiable, use the phrase *of the* after your qualifier.
- If the quantifier precedes articles (a/an/the), demonstratives (this/that/these/those), or possessive determiners (my/your/our), it is always followed by *of*.
- The verb agrees in number with the noun that follows the quantifier. Note: *one, each,* and *every* normally take singular verbs, whether or not they are followed by *of*.

  Examples:

  One of the provinces is on the West coast. (singular countable noun)

  Several of the provinces are on the Canadian Shield. (plural countable noun)

  Some of this water is polluted. (uncountable)

  Some of my relatives live on the coast. (plural countable noun)

Commonly Confused Quantifiers:

1. *A few* and *a little* vs. *few* and *little*

   Examples:

   There are a few people camping. (people = countable noun)

Please give me a little maple syrup (maple syrup = uncountable noun)

Few people go camping in the winter. (people = countable noun)

Little work gets done during snowstorms. (work = uncountable noun)

Few and *little* have the same grammatical function as *a few* and *a little* but their meaning is different. *Few* and *little* indicate that there is not enough of something or it is not easy to get. *A few* and *a little* mean a small amount.

Few and *little* are the formal versions of *not many* and *not much*.

2. *Many* and *much* (and *lots of / a lot of*)

Many and *much* in the affirmative are considered formal while *lots of / a lot of* are informal

Lots of / a lot of can be used with both countable and uncountable nouns.

3. *Some* and *any* with plural and uncountable nouns

Some is used in affirmative statements and *any* is used in questions and negatives.

   Examples:

   I have some questions.

   Do you have any questions?

   I don't have any questions.

Unit 4: Stay Tuned!

Reported Speech

We use reported speech to say what someone has said in the past. We may report what we heard in a conversation, what someone has told us, or what we read in an interview.

In some situations we may want to use the exact words of the original speaker. In writing, we use quotation marks around the original speaker's words to show that these are the exact words of the speaker. This makes it clear that although we are reporting the sentence, the words are not ours. In speaking, we usually use a reported speech form.

Often we report the gist of what someone has said rather than the exact words. In these cases, we do not use quotations marks. We use an indirect (reported) speech form.

Direct quote: "I'm eating cereal with yogourt for breakfast."

Reported speech: The TV star said that she was eating cereal with yogourt for breakfast.

Changes in pronouns

In order to show that the person who said the original words is not the same person who is reporting the words, we change the pronouns of the original sentence. In the example above, *I* refers to the female TV star, not the person who is reporting what the star said. Therefore, in the reported speech, we change the pronoun *I* to *she* or use the noun phrase *the TV star* to make the meaning clear. Let the meaning of the sentence guide your decision about changing pronouns.

Changes in tense

A second way to make it clear that the words we are speaking were said by someone else is to change the tense of the verbs in the original statement. The original speech was said at a different time than the reported speech.

On Tuesday morning Lola says:	"I'm eating cereal with yogourt for breakfast."
On Wednesday afternoon Lola's friend reports what Lola said:	She said (that) she was eating cereal with yogourt for breakfast.

Because Lola was eating this food on Tuesday morning but not on Wednesday, when it was reported, we change the present time frame of the original to the past time frame in the reported speech to show the time difference. Note: the word *that* is optional.

When you want to show the time difference, use one tense back in the past from the original tense.

From past to past perfect

Original	Simple past	"I *didn't put* a photo of my lunch on Facebook."
Reported	Past perfect	He said he *hadn't put* a photo of his lunch on Facebook.
Original	Past continuous	"I *was checking* my email."
Reported	Past perfect continuous	He said he *had been checking* his email.

From present to past

Original	Simple present	"I *check* Facebook every day."
Reported	Simple past	He said he *checked* Facebook every day.
Original	Present continuous	"I'*m reading* a tweet from my favourite movie star."
Reported	Past continuous	He said he *was reading* a tweet from his favourite movie star.
Original	Present perfect	"His dad has *started* downloading music from iTunes."
Reported	Past perfect	He said his dad had *started* downloading music from iTunes.
Original	Present perfect continuous	"I've *been following* this celebrity for a month."
Reported	Past perfect continuous	He said he'd *been following* this celebrity for a month.

Changes in tense are not always necessary

- The verb tense in an original statement remains unchanged if the state of affairs still exists when the speech is reported.

Direct quote: "I'm going to buy the new version of the game when it comes on the market next month."

Reported speech: She said she's going to buy the new version of the game when it comes on the market next month.

- When the simple present tense in an original statement is used to mean a general fact, a habit, or an unspecified time, the tense in the reported speech does not have to change, especially if the original information is still relevant.

  Direct quote: "I like cereal with yogourt for breakfast."

  Reported speech: The TV star said that she likes cereal with yogourt for breakfast.

- Past tenses in an original statement may remain unchanged (especially in spoken English) if there is no confusion about the time of the original action.

  Direct quote: "The musician performed in Winnipeg on Monday."

  Reported speech: He said the musician performed in Winnipeg on Monday.

  OR

  He said the musician had performed in Winnipeg on Monday.

Reporting Questions

1. In reported questions, the reporting verb changes to *asked* and the sentence ends with a period, not a question mark, because the speaker who is reporting the question is not asking the question.

2. We use the same rules for changing pronouns and tenses when we report questions, but there are two additional changes.

   a) Add the word *if* to mark that the original sentence was a *yes/no* question. Use the same *wh* question word as in the direct quote to mark that the original question was an information question.

      Direct quote: "Do you eat breakfast in the morning?"

      Reported speech: The interviewer asked *if* she ate breakfast in the morning.

      Direct quote: "Why do you tweet?"

      Reported speech: The interviewer asked *why* I tweeted.

   b) Change the word order to a statement word order, not a question word order.

- When the question word is in the object position of the sentence, follow this word order:

A. Verb *to be*

Direct Quote	Reported Question	question word +	subject	+ verb + . . .
Where is my laptop?	She asked	where	my laptop	was.
When was the movie star here?	She asked	when	the movie star	was here.
Why was your computer on?	She asked	why	my computer	was on.
Who is the writer?	She asked	who	the writer	was.
What is his name?	She asked	what	his name	was.

B. Other Verbs

Direct Quote	Reported Question	question word +	subject	+ verb + . . .
When did you download that game?	She asked	when	I	downloaded that game.
Why does he tweet?	She asked	why	he	tweeted.
Where did they go?	She asked	where	they	went.
When will the movie start?	She asked	when	the movie	would start.
What did the celebrity say?	She asked	what	the celebrity	said.

When *Who or What* are in the subject position of the sentence, follow this word order:

A. Verb *to be*

Direct Quote	Reported Question		
	question word + verb + . . .		
	(subject)		
Who is interested in blogging?	She asked who	was	interested in blogging.
Who is responsible for this site?	She asked who	was	responsible for this site.
What is playing at the cinema?	She asked what	was	playing at the cinema.
What is popular in music?	She asked what	was	popular in music.

B. Other Verbs

Direct Quote	**Reported Question**		
	question word + verb + . . .		
	(subject)		
Who recorded that song?	She asked who	recorded	that song.
What caused the breakup?	She asked what	caused	the breakup.
Who performed last night?	She asked who	performed	last night.
What interests them?	She asked what	interested	them.

Reporting sentences with modals

The rules about changing tenses also apply to modals used in the present tense:

may ⟶ might
can ⟶ could
will ⟶ would

Direct quote: "I <u>won't</u> come to the bar on Tuesday night."

Reported speech: Hal's friend said he <u>wouldn't</u> come to the bar on Tuesday night.

Note: Do not change past modals to past perfect modals.

Unit 5: Buyer Beware!

Gerunds and Gerund Phrases

A gerund is a verbal that indicates an action or state of being. A verbal is a verb form, but it does not act like a verb in a sentence—it functions as a noun. A gerund can have the same position in the sentence as other nouns. It can be a subject, a direct object, or an object of a preposition. A gerund phrase contains the object of the gerund or any words used to modify it.

1. The gerund can be the subject of the sentence. The gerund in the subject position is always singular. The gerund can be replaced by the pronoun *it*.

   Example:

   > subject
   >
   > <u>Purchasing a computer</u> is expensive. (gerund + modifier + V)

   > <u>It</u> is expensive.

2. The gerund can be the subject complement.

   Example:

   > subject complement
   >
   > His favourite activity is <u>listening to music</u>. (S + be + gerund)

3. The gerund can be the object of certain verbs. There is no pattern or rule—you need to memorize these verbs. See the following chart for a list.

Examples:

I dislike purchasing extended warranties. (S + V + gerund)

I recommend researching the product before going to the store.

4. The gerund (G) *always* follows a preposition (P) if you want to indicate an action or a state of being. It is the object of the preposition.

Examples:

   V + P   G

I plan on purchasing a television. (S + phrasal verb + gerund)

      V + P   G

I believe in remaining positive at all times. (S + phrasal verb + gerund)

Verbs Followed by the Gerund

Verbs that indicate that something is starting, finishing, or is incomplete:	Verbs about communication:	Verbs about a continuing action:
avoid	admit	can't help
begin	advise	practice
delay	deny	
finish	discuss	
postpone	mention	
quit	recommend	
risk	report	
	suggest	
Verbs about emotion:	**Verbs about thinking:**	
appreciate	consider	
enjoy	imagine	
mind	understand	
don't mind		
regret		
resist		
tolerate		

Common Verbs Followed by a Preposition and a Gerund

admit to	disapprove of	prevent (someone) from
approve of	discourage from	refrain from
argue about	dream about	succeed in
believe in	feel like	talk about
care about	forget about	think about
complain about	insist on	worry about
concentrate on	keep on	give up
confess to	object to	
depend on	plan on	

Spelling Rules for Forming the Gerund

Add *–ing* to the base form of the verb (e.g., watch—watching)

- If the verb ends with an *e*, drop the *e* and add *–ing* (e.g., purchase—purchasing)

- If the last three letters are a consonant-vowel-consonant (CVC) pattern, double the last consonant and add *–ing* (e.g., hit—hitting). In verbs with two or more syllables, follow this rule only if the last syllable is stressed (e.g., oc/cur—occurring; o/pen—opening).

Note: If the verb ends in *w*, *x*, or *y*, do not double the last consonant (e.g., pay—paying).

- If the verb ends in –*ie*, change the *ie* to *y* before adding –*ing* (e.g., die—dying).

Unit 6: Catch Me If You Can

The Passive Voice

In English, an action is expressed by the verb in the sentence. Sometimes we want to emphasize who or what performed the action. In this case, we use active voice. Other times we want to emphasize the action itself. In this case, we use passive voice. We build the sentence differently, depending on what we want to emphasize.

ACTIVE:

subject (*doer of the action*)	verb (*action*)	object (*receiver of action*)
The investigator	collected	the trace evidence.

PASSIVE:

subject (*receiver of action*)	verb (*action*)	object of *by* phrase (*doer of the action*)
The trace evidence	was collected	by the investigator.

Both of the sentences contain the same information. However, each sentence emphasizes a different part of the information.

Use passive voice…

- to emphasize the receiver of the action rather than the doer:

  Example:

  The crime scene was photographed systematically.

- to describe a situation in which the doer of the action is unknown or unimportant:

  Example:

  Over thirty pieces of important evidence were stored at the police station.

- when the identity of the person doing the action is obvious:

  Example:

  He was arrested on suspicion of selling drugs.

Forming The Passive Voice

To form a passive sentence, put the verb *be* in the same tense as the active verb and add the V3 form of the active verb.

ACTIVE: The police *arrested* the suspect. (simple past tense)

PASSIVE: The suspect *was arrested* by the police. (verb *be* in simple past tense + V₃)

Tense	Active Voice	Passive Voice *be* + V_2
simple present	robs	is robbed
simple past	robbed	was robbed
future	will rob	will be robbed
modal + V_1	might rob	might be robbed

Note:

S + be + V_3: The thieves were caught.

S + be + not + V_3: The thieves were not caught.

Be + S + V_3? Were the thieves caught?

Be + S + not + V_3? Were the thieves not caught?

Be + not + S + V_3? Weren't the thieves caught?

wh– word + be + not + S + V_3? Why weren't the thieves caught?

General Rules

In general, we prefer to use the active. Here are some rules about the passive voice:

- Only active sentences that contain an object may be put into the passive voice.

- The object of the active sentence becomes the subject of the passive sentence. The subject of the active sentence becomes the object of the *by* phrase.

- The *by* phrase is often omitted. Use it only when you want to tell who or what the agent is, especially if it is unexpected.

Unit 7: Doing the Right Thing

Real and Unreal Conditionals

We use conditional sentences to show condition/result relationships. If the condition happens or is true, the result will also happen or be true.

Example:

If you lie to your friends, they will not trust you anymore.

condition	**result**

If there is a real possibility that the condition will happen (in the present situation), then the conditional sentence is real. If it is impossible or unlikely that the condition will happen (in the present situation), then the conditional sentence is unreal. Whether the condition is real or unreal depends on the situation in which the sentence is said.

Example:

Real: If the teacher catches Jeff cheating on the test, she will give him a zero.

(It is possible that the teacher will catch Jeff cheating.)

Unreal: If Jeff broke into the teacher's office and stole the test answers, he would get a perfect score.

(It is very unlikely that Jeff will break into the teacher's office.)

Placement of the if clause

A conditional sentence has an independent clause (the result clause) and a dependent clause (the *if* clause). An *if* clause cannot stand alone as a complete sentence.

The dependent *if* clause can come before or after the independent result clause. The position of the *if* clause does not change the meaning of the sentence.

- When the dependent *if* clause comes before the independent result clause, we separate the clauses with a comma.

Example:

If it were legal, Henry would do it.

- We do not separate the clauses with a comma when the independent result clause comes before the dependent *if* clause.

Example:

Henry would do it *if it were legal.*

Tenses in Real and Unreal Conditionals
Real Conditionals

In real conditional sentences, the normal rules for tenses apply. We use tenses as we do in any other English sentence.

Unreal Conditionals

In unreal conditional sentences, we have a different rule. We need to signal that the condition is unreal, so we put the tense of the verbs in the *if* clause and the result clause in a past form. These past tense verbs do not mean the condition happened in the past. It means that the condition is unreal.

	Real Conditional	Unreal Conditional
present or future condition	If you **lie** to your friends, they **will not trust** you anymore.	If you **stole** a car, the police **would arrest** you.
	(It's possible that you lie or will lie to your friends.)	(It's unlikely that you will steal a car.)

Note: Even though the condition in the *if* clause has not happened yet, we do not put the verb in the *if* clause in a future tense.

Real Conditional

If + S + V₁...,	*S + will V....*
If we treat the employees fairly,	they will trust us.
If you are honest,	people will trust you.

If + S + do/does + NOT +V...,	*S + will V....*
If they don't behave ethically,	they will feel guilty.
If he doesn't value honesty,	he will lie.

If + S + be (V_1) *+ NOT . . .*	*S + will V. . . .*
If she isn't lying	I will feel better.
Wh + will +S + V . . .	*if + S +* V_1 *. . .?*
What will you do	if he lies to you?
Will + S + V. . .	*if + S +* V_1 *. . .?*
Will you respect him	if he treats you unfairly?

Unreal Conditional

If + S + V_2 *. . .,*	*S + would V. . . .*
If you bribed a police officer,	you would be untrustworthy.
*If the employee were corrupt,	I would report him to the management.
If + S + did + NOT +V_1*. . .,*	*S + would V. . . .*
If she didn't feel guilty about lying,	I would be disappointed.
If + S + were + NOT. . .,	*S + would V. . . .*
*If the employee weren't corrupt,	I would trust her.
Wh– + would +S + V_1	*if + S +* V_2 *(or were) . . .?*
What would they do	if their child stole something?
What would you do	if you were in this situation?*
Would + S + V_1*. . .*	*if + S +* V_2 *(or were) . . .?*
Would you trust her	if she lied to you?
Would you lie	if you were in this situation?*

*use *were* for the verb *be* in the unreal conditional

Unit 8: Love Is in the Air!

Adjective Clauses

An adjective clause is a dependent clause. It has a subject and predicate, but it is not a complete idea. It needs another part of the sentence to complete its idea. An adjective clause is used in the same way as a single adjective or adjective phrase. It describes a noun (person, place, thing, or idea).

Placement of the Adjective Clause

Adjective clauses usually follow the nouns they modify. They can be found in the various sentence positions depending on the location of the noun they are describing.

- An adjective clause can modify a noun in the object position of the sentence.

  Example:

  I used to date <u>a woman</u> *who lived in Sri Lanka.*
  object — adjective clause

- An adjective clause can modify a noun in the subject position of the sentence.

  Example:

  <u>The bottle of wine</u> *that was on the table* was excellent.
  subject — adjective clause

Note: When *who* or *what* is the subject of the adjective clause, you don't need to add another subject.

Sheila wants *a man* who ~~he~~ has   a sense of humour.

$$\underbrace{\text{subject} + \text{verb} + \text{object}}_{\text{adjective clause}}$$

They want *a honeymoon* that ~~it~~ is   exciting.

$$\underbrace{\text{subject} + \text{verb} + \text{adjective}}_{\text{adjective clause}}$$

S + V + O + (who/that + V . . .)
She wants a man who likes expensive things.

S + aux + NOT + V + O + (who/that + V . . .)
She doesn't want a man who likes expensive things.

aux + S + V + O + (who/that + V . . .)?
Does she want a man who likes expensive things?

Wh– + aux + S + V + O + (who/that + V . . .)?
Why does she want a man who likes expensive things?

Unit 9: Get Those Creative Juices Flowing!

Information Questions

- *Why* questions ask for reasons.

- *How* questions ask about the way in which something is done.

- *Where* questions ask about places.

  A place can be a physical location, but it can also be an origin.

  Examples:

  a) <u>Where</u> did da Vinci live?
  He lived <u>in Italy.</u>

  b) <u>Where </u>did Google get its name? (What is the origin of the name?)

  Google is a misspelling of the word "googolplex," which means a large amount of information.

- *When* questions ask about time.

  We can express time as a phrase.

  Example:

  <u>When</u> is the concert?
  The concert is <u>on Saturday</u>.

We can also express time as a clause.

Example:

<u>When</u> should a working group use the Six Hats technique?

It should use the techniques <u>when it needs to solve a problem</u>.

- *Who* questions ask about people.

  a) *Who* as subject:

  Example:

  <u>Who</u> wrote that song?
  <u>Leonard Cohen</u> wrote that song.

  b) *Who* as object:

  Example:

  <u>Who(m)</u> did you sing with?
  I sang with <u>my friend</u>.

Note: When *who* is the object of the sentence, it formally becomes *whom*. However, people usually say *who*.

Don't confuse *who's* and *whose*.
- *Who's* is the short form of *who is* or *who has*.
  Example:
  Who's the artist?
- *Whose* is a possessive pronoun.
  Example:
  Whose paintings are these? (They're mine.)

- *What* questions ask about all other information

  a) *What* as subject:

  Example:

  <u>What</u> develops curiosity?
  <u>Asking questions</u> develops curiosity.

  b) What as object:

  Example:

  <u>What</u> do creative people do?
  Creative people <u>ask lots of questions</u>.

	verb *be* *Wh–* + be + S	other verbs *Wh–* + V + S
Who	Who is the artist? Who was the writer?	Who reads science fiction? Who wrote the song?
		Wh– + auxiliary/modal + NOT + S Who doesn't like opera?
	Wh– + be + S	*Wh–* + auxiliary/modal + S + V
What	What was the name of the song?	What do creative people do?
Where	Where is the concert?	Where can we buy the tickets?
When	When was the concert?	When did the concert begin?
Why	Why are you here?	Why did he write that poem?
How	How are you?	How can we develop our creative potential? *Wh–* + aux/modal + NOT + S + V Why don't we buy the tickets online? What didn't they see at the museum?

Unit 10: That's So Canadian

Articles

One way to give more information about a noun is to use an article (the, a/an). Articles tell us whether or not the noun is specific and identifiable in the situation.

- Articles always come before the noun, never after (e.g., a tourist).
- Articles are always in the first position of a noun phrase (e.g., the curious tourist).
- When using *a/an*, use *an* if the word that follows begins with a vowel sound, except if the vowel sound is a /juː/ (e.g., a university, a uniform). If a word begins with a silent *h*, it follows the vowel sound rule (e.g., an honour). Use *a* if the word that follows begins with a consonant sound.

Deciding which article to use

Before you can make a decision about which article to use, you must know two things about the noun.

1. Is the noun countable (e.g., airplane) or uncountable (e.g., wind)?
2. Is the noun unspecified (indefinite) or specified (definite)?

Unspecified (indefinite) nouns

With an unspecified noun, the reader or listener does not know exactly which *one* or *ones* you mean by the noun.

Example:

I met a tourist on the bus. (Which tourist? The reader or listener does not know the specific tourist. It could be any tourist on the bus.)

Specified (definite) nouns

With a specified noun, the reader or listener can imagine or assume exactly which noun you are talking about.

Example:

The tourist I met on the bus yesterday was from India. (Which tourist? The reader or listener knows that it is the tourist you met yesterday on the bus who is from India.)

There are many complex rules for deciding which article to use, but a few of the most important are included in the chart below.

General Rules for Articles

Use A/An

- Use *a/an* before a noun that is singular, countable, and unspecified (e.g., a Russian immigrant).
- Use *a/an* in expressions of measurement where the meaning is *each* (e.g., five days a week).
- Do not use *a/an* before a plural noun.
- Do not use *a/an* before a noun that is uncountable.

Use The

- Use *the* before a noun that was introduced earlier in the text with the article *a/an*.
- Use *the* before a noun if the noun was made definite in an earlier sentence.
- Use *the* before any noun that refers to a specific person or thing.
- Use *the* with superlative forms or adjectives that come before a noun (e.g., the greatest sport).
- Use *the* with any adjective or participle that is used as a noun (e.g., the poor, the hungry).
- Use *the* with the following proper nouns: rivers (e.g., the Mackenzie River), mountain ranges (e.g., the Rocky Mountains), oceans (e.g., the Pacific Ocean), monuments and buildings (e.g., the CN Tower), geographical regions (e.g., the Prairies), and political/economic unions (e.g., the European Union).
- Do not use *the* before a proper noun that refers to a person (e.g., Maurice Richard), language (e.g., French), country (e.g., Canada), or lake (e.g., Lake Ontario), but use *the* before a language that is named (e.g., the English language).
- Do not use *the* before a noun that is used as a general idea.

Use Ø (no article)

- Don't use articles (a/an, the) with plural nouns that are unspecified.
- Don't use articles (a/an, the) with nouns that are uncountable and unspecified.
- Don't use articles (a/an, the) with nouns that talk about general ideas or concepts.
- Don't use the indefinite article (a/an) with plurals or uncountable nouns.

Chapter 4

Pronunciation Power, Exercise D

Partner A should read either sentence a or b of each pair to Partner B.

6. a) More than three-quarters of US people eighteen to twenty say they read a daily newspaper on an average day.

   b) More than a quarter of US people eighteen to twenty-two say they read a daily newspaper on an average day.

7. a) Worldwide, ninety-two percent of people surveyed said they use email to communicate with friends and family.

   b) Worldwide, ninety percent of people surveyed said they use email to communicate with friends and family.

8. a) Nearly sixteen percent of online adults worldwide have made friends using the Internet and have an average of forty-one online friends.

   b) Nearly sixty percent of online adults worldwide have made friends using the Internet and have an average of forty-one online friends.

9. a) Forty percent of adults have restarted romantic relationships online, especially in India (thirty-seven percent) and Brazil (twenty five percent).

   b) Fourteen percent of adults have restarted romantic relationships online, especially in India (thirty-seven percent) and Brazil (twenty-five percent).

10. a) In the US, approximately a third of youth eighteen to twenty say they read a newspaper on a Sunday.

    b) In the US, approximately two-thirds of youth eighteen to twenty say they read a newspaper on a Sunday.

Target Academic Word List (AWL) words per unit

Words on the list are as they appear in the text. Where the word in the text is in a different grammatical form than the AWL headword, the headword is included in parentheses.

Unit 1

altered	job	recover
attribute	motivate (motive)	series
elements	physical	source
generated		

Unit 2

consequently (consequent)	evidence	professional
construction (construct)	expert	projects
designers (design)	identity	require
ethnic		

Unit 3

area	financial (finance)	participating (participate)
brief	immigrants (immigrate)	ranges (range)
debate	major	reveals
exposed		

Unit 4

access	percent	tasks
communicate	role	technology
data	survey	traditional (tradition)
overall		

Unit 5

assume	purchase	strategies
contacts	register	targets (target)
individual	specifically (specific)	transfer
item		

Unit 6

analysis (analyze)	index	previously (previous)
approximately (approximate)	occurred	removes
estimate	period	security (secure)
images		

Unit 7

available
commit
computer (compute)
conclusion (conclude)

consumer (consume)
distributed
final

focus
tape
technique

Unit 8

approach
appropriate
attitudes
challenge

consulted
involving (involve)
mentality (mental)

methods
normal
partners

Unit 9

affects (affect)
creativity (create)
demonstrate
energy

environments
perspective
potential

principles
research
relies

Unit 10

chapters
cultures
defining (define)
economic (economy)

goals
issues
location (locate)

process
sections
statistics

Literary Credits

6 Historica Minute: "Superman." Historica Dominion Institute; 18 "Lost Treasure of the Knights Templar," *Unexplained*; 36 "Canadian Railroad Trilogy," by Gordon Lightfoot; 38–44 GFK's Roper Reports Worldwide study (statistics/graphs); 40–44 The Nielsen Company; 45 Norton Online Living Report Survey, 2009; Symantec Corporation ©2009; 45 Harris Interactive Trends & Tudes, Vol 8, Issue 3 July 2009 for graph, Norton Online; 60–61 The YGS Group; 62 © Copyright 2010, Her Majesty the Queen in Right of Canada as represented by the Royal Canadian Mounted Police; 68 Settlement.org "How do I make a consumer complaint?" Copyright © 2009 Ontario Council of Agencies Serving Immigrants (OCASI); 77 Source: Adapted from Statistics Canada. "Victims and Persons Accused of Homicide in Canada, by age and sex" Available online; 82 Amnesty International Canada; 85–86 "Music Piracy: Is downloading music ethical?" Helium.com; 103–105 Anand Ram; 106 Citizen and Immigration Canada; 122 Canadian Broadcasting Corporation; 137–138 Copyright Shayne Koyczan.

Photograph Credits

1 Mark Divers/iStock International Inc; 2 (tl) Spider-Man and all other Marvel characters: TM © 2010 Marvel Entertainment, LLC and its subsidiaries. All Rights Reserved., (br) Ham/CartoonStock; 3 Copyright DC Comics; 5 Kes/CartoonStock; 10 Seon Winn/iStock International Inc; 11 Karen Moller/iStock International Inc; 12 (l) Digital Vision (c) Jarno Gonzalez Zarraonandia/iStock International Inc, (r) Daniel Padavona/iStock International Inc; 13 (l) Clipart.com, (c) Manuel Velasco/iStock International Inc, (r) © Charles & Josette Lenars/Corbis; 14 (t) Joze Pojbic/iStock International Inc, (c) Copyright Sagalassos Archaeological Research Project; 16 Maxx Images; 17 (bl) Propix/Dreamstime, (br) G. Casillas; 18 Roccomontoya/iStock International Inc; 20 (t) Eduardo Antonio Fuentes/iStock International Inc, (c) Jonathan Hill/iStock International Inc; 22 (t)Pawel Gaul/iStock International Inc, (c) Julie de Leseleuc/iStock International Inc, (b) Ryerson Clark/iStock International Inc; 23 (t-b) Andrea Gingerich/iStock International Inc, Philipp Maitz/iStock International Inc, Björn Kindler/iStock International Inc, Canadian Broadcasting Corporation, biffspandex/iStock International Inc; 24 *The Regional geography of Canada, Fourth Edition*, Martin Bone; 25 (t) Neta Degany/iStock International Inc (b) Michael Olson/iStock International Inc; 26 (t) Cynthia Baldauf/iStock International Inc, (b) Andrew Penner/iStock International Inc; 27 (t) Gaetane Harvey/iStock International Inc, (b) (c) Rich Thomas. Image from BigStockPhoto.com; 28 (t-b) Copyright Robert Bateman. By arrangement with the Ansada Group, LLC., Maxx Images, WO Mitchell - For more information on W.O. Mitchell, visit www.womitchell.ca, Courtesy of the Estate of the late Dr. Naomi Jackson Groves, Corel; 29 isifa/Getty Images Entertainment; 33 Clipart.com; 34 Alexander Gocotano/iStock International Inc; 41 Magdalena Tworkowska/iStock International Inc; 44 mimonbear/iStock International Inc; 48 (tl) Used with the permission of Joel Pett and the Cartoonist Group. All rights reserved.,(tr)Shane Obrien/iStock International Inc (cl) 9Lives/iStock International Inc; 51 (c) Chris Schmidt/iStock International Inc, (b) drbimages/iStock International Inc; 52 (tl) KAP, (tr) Clipart.com (bl) Matt Hamm (br) Kim Boyle—caricaturist/cartoonist; 55 Florea Marius Catalin/iStock International Inc; 57 zorani/iStock International Inc; 58 Camilla Wisbauer/iStock International Inc; 60 Denis Pepin/iStock International Inc; 61 (tr) David Schmidt/iStock International Inc (cl) Roberto Saporito/iStock International Inc (br) Alex Slobodkin/iStock International Inc; 62 ktsimage/iStock International Inc; 69 Dmitriy Shironosov/iStock International Inc; 70 (t) Darren Mower/iStock International Inc (cl-cr) UpperCut, Giorgio Fochesato/iStock International Inc, Eddie Green/iStock International Inc, (b) Photodisc; 72 bigredlynx/iStock International Inc; 74 (l) Hans Laubel/iStock International Inc (c) Andrew Brown/iStock International Inc (r) Dan Van Oss/iStock International Inc; 75 Comstock; 80 *Oxford Picture Dictionary Second Edition* by Jayme Adelson-Goldstein and Norma Shapiro © Oxford University Press 2008; 83 Calvin and Hobbes copyright Universal Uclick; 84 (t) Josef Philipp/iStock International Inc (b) Leigh Schindler/iStock International Inc; 87 liangpv/iStock International Inc; 89 Robyn Mackenzie/iStock International Inc; 96 Andrew Rich/iStock International Inc; 99 Mark Wragg/iStock International Inc; 100 (tl-tr) Photodisc, PhotoAlto /Alamy, Digital Vision, Photodisc; (c) Shane Obrien/iStock International Inc; (bl-br) Photodisc, John Foxx, Photodisc, Ingram; 101 (tl-tr) Photodisc, Photodisc, Photodisc, John Foxx (bl-br) Roman Milert/Big Stock Photo, Photodisc, Digital Vision, PhotoAlto/Alamy; 103 Umbar Shakir/iStock International Inc; 109 CartoonStock; 113 Vanda Grigorovic/iStock International Inc; 114 (t)Paul Fleet/Big Stock Photo; 115 (tl) Ember Stefano/Maxx Images (tr) Copyright Morris Architects (b) Ilian Car; 116 Ivan Burmistrov/iStock International Inc; 117 John Woodcock/iStock International Inc; 118 (l) Giacomo Nodari/Dreamstime, (r) Photographers Choice; 119 (t) T-Immagini/iStock International Inc (b) DNY59/iStock International Inc; 120 Luca di Filippo/iStock International Inc; 125 (l) Eimantas Buzas/iStock International Inc (r) Tim Robberts/Getty Images; 126 Genevieve Sang, gensang@gmail.com, 126(r)–127(l) Jaimie Duplass/iStock International Inc; 127–128 Steve Dangers iStock International Inc; 129 DJ Art/Image Envision; 130 (tl-cr) Tim Horton's is a registered trade mark of the TDL Marks Corporation. Used with permission, Canadian Tire Money reproduced with permission of Canadian Tire, Sergey Borisov/iStock International Inc, biffspandex/iStock International Inc, First Light/Alamy, Frank Leung/iStock International Inc, Eric Isselée/iStock International Inc, David Goldman/Contour, Domen Blenkus/iStock International Inc, (b) Saul Herrera/iStock International Inc; 139 bubaone/iStock International Inc